Emmett Dulaney

MCSE
FAST TRACK
Internet
Information
Server 4

New
Riders

201 West 103rd Street, Indianapolis, Indiana 46290

MCSE FAST TRACK:
INTERNET INFORMATION
SERVER 4

International Standard Book Number: 1-56205-936-X

Library of Congress Catalog Card Number: 98-86319

Printed in the United States of America

First Printing: September, 1998

00 99 98   4 3 2 1

TRADEMARKS

WARNING AND DISCLAIMER

Executive Editor
Mary Foote

Acquisitions Editor
Steve Weiss

Development Editor
Nancy Warner

Managing Editor
Sarah Kearns

Project Editor
Clint McCarty

Copy Editor
Kate Givens

Indexer
John Sleeva

Technical Editors
Andrew Brice
Grant Jones

Book Designers
Nathan Clement
Ruth Lewis

Cover Designer
Sandra Schroeder

Production
Cheryl Lynch
Megan Wade

Contents at a Glance

TABLE OF CONTENTS

ABOUT THE AUTHOR

Emmett Dulaney, MCP+I, MCSE is a consultant for D S Technical Solutions, and instructor for a national training company. He has been teaching certification courses for the continuing education department of Indiana University/Purdue University at Fort Wayne for over four years, and is the Certification Corner columnist for *NT Systems Magazine*. In addition, Emmett is the author or coauthor of over a dozen computer books, including *CNE Short Course, Sams Teach Yourself MCSE Windows NT Workstation in 14 Days,* and *MCSE TestPrep: TCP/IP.* He has also written over 100 magazine articles on computing for several publications.

ABOUT THE TECHNICAL EDITORS

R. Andrew Brice currently works as a senior instructor for ProSoft I-Net Solutions in Austin, Texas. His certifications include Novell CNA and CNE, as well as the Microsoft Certified Trainer and Microsoft Certified Systems Engineer in both Windows NT 3.51 and 4.0. Since 1991, he has been providing consulting in network design and support to small and large organizations, including Fortune 1000 companies. This consulting has included training for Novell, Microsoft, and Netscape technical curricula, coupled with Web site development, security, and e-commerce. He specializes in the design and implementation of wide area networks (WAN). He credits his accomplishments to the love and support provided by both his wife, Susan, and his daughter, Katie. He can be reached at andrewb@flash.net.

Grant Jones has worked as a network engineer for the past five years, and is certified as an MCSE, MCP + Inet, MCT, CNE3/4 (Certified NetWare Engineer versions 3 and 4), and CNI (Certified NetWare Instructor). For the past three years, Grant has been teaching the official Microsoft core classes along with IIS and TCP/IP; he is currently working for ProSoft I-Net Solutions, where he is creating courseware for ePC certifications. Grant has written courses on Netscape Mail and IIS 4.0; the course he developed on IIS 4.0 was taught to Microsoft Visual Basic programmers in Redmond, WA. In addition, Grant has spoken at trade shows such as Internet World and Internet Commerce Expo on Internet fundamentals and electronic commerce.

DEDICATION

For Karen.

ACKNOWLEDGMENTS

First and foremost, I would like to thank Steve Weiss for his conviction and belief in the product and for his patience with it, as well. I would also like to thank Nancy Warner, Andrew Brice, Grant Jones, and Clint McCarty.

TELL US WHAT YOU THINK!

As the reader of this book, *you* are our most important critic and commentator. We value your opinion and want to know what we're doing right, what we could do better, what areas you'd like to see us publish in, and any other words of wisdom you're willing to pass our way.

As the Executive Editor for the Certification team at Macmillan Computer Publishing, I welcome your comments. You can fax, email, or write me directly to let me know what you did or didn't like about this book—as well as what we can do to make our books stronger.

Please note that I cannot help you with technical problems related to the topic of this book, and that due to the high volume of mail I receive, I might not be able to reply to every message.

When you write, please be sure to include this book's title and author, as well as your name and phone or fax number. I will carefully review your comments and share them with the author and editors who worked on the book.

Fax:	317-581-4663
Email:	certification@mcp.com
Mail:	Mary Foote
	Executive Editor
	Certification
	Macmillan Computer Publishing
	201 West 103rd Street
	Indianapolis, IN 46290

Introduction

The *MCSE Fast Track* series is written as a study aid for people preparing for Microsoft Certification Exams. The series is intended to help reinforce and clarify information with which the student is already familiar. This series is not intended to be a single source for student preparation, but rather a review of information and set of practice materials to help increase the likelihood of success when taking the actual exam.

WHY WE DID THIS SERIES: WORDS FROM THE AUTHOR AND PUBLISHER

First, let's state this once more: New Riders' *MCSE Fast Tracks* are not intended to be single sources for exam preparation. These books have been uniquely written and developed to work as supplements to your existing knowledge base.

But exactly what makes them different?

1. **Brevity.** Many other exam training materials seek Microsoft approval (you've probably seen the official "Microsoft Approved Study Guide" logo on other books, for example), meaning they must include 50% tutorial material and cover every objective for every exam in exactly the same manner, to the same degree. *MCSE Fast Tracks break away from that mold by focusing on what you really need to know to pass the exams.*

2. **Focus.** Fast Tracks are targeted primarily to those who know the technology but who don't yet have the certification. No superfluous information is included. *MCSE Fast Tracks* feature only what the more-experienced candidate needs to know to pass the exams. *Fast Tracks are affordable study material for the experienced professional.*

3. **Concentrated value and learning power.** Frankly, we wouldn't be surprised if Fast Tracks prove to appeal to a wider audience than just advanced-level candidates. We've tried to pack as much distilled exam knowledge as possible into *Fast Tracks*, creating a

"digest" of exam-critical information. No matter what level you're at, you may see this digest on certification training as a logical starting point for exam study.

4. **Classroom-tested, instructor-proven.** With tens of thousands of new certification candidates entering the training routine each year, trainers like Emmett Dulaney—on the forefront of the certification education lines—are finding themselves in front of classes comprised of increased numbers of candidates with the following:

   ◆ already a measurable base of understanding of the technology

   ◆ a desire for efficient, "just-the-facts" training

Emmett and New Riders pooled their thoughts and found that no books *truly* existed that adequately fill this need:

To provide an easy way to review the key elements of each certification technology without being bogged down with elementary-level information and to present this information in the light of an insider's perspective.

Emmett developed his instructional style and content to help this ever-increasing group of nonbeginners, and they in turn helped him focus the material even more. He then worked with New Riders to develop this classroom-tested material into a refined, efficient self-instruction tool. What you see in this book is the result of that interaction.

Think of *Fast Tracks* as the set of instructor's notes you always wished you could get your hands on. These notes only truly help you if you already know the material and are ready to take on the exam itself. It's then that this book is truly designed to help you shine. Good luck and may your hard work pay off.

WHO SHOULD READ THIS BOOK

The Internet Information Server 4 book in the *MCSE Fast Track* series is specifically intended to help students prepare for Microsoft's Implementing and Supporting Microsoft Internet Information Server 4.0 (70-087) exam, one of the elective options in the MCSE program.

PART I: WHAT THE IIS EXAM (70-087) COVERS

The Implementing and Supporting Microsoft Internet Information Server 4.0 certification exam measures your ability to implement, administer, and troubleshoot computer systems that are running Microsoft Internet Information Server 4.0. It focuses on determining your skill in seven major categories. These categories follow:

- Planning
- Installation and Configuration
- Configuring and Managing Resource Access
- Integration and Interoperability
- Running Applications
- Monitoring and Optimization
- Troubleshooting

The Implementing and Supporting Microsoft Internet Information Server 4.0 certification exam uses these categories to measure your ability. Before taking this exam, you should be proficient in the job skills discussed in the following pages.

Planning

The Planning section is designed to make sure that you understand the hardware requirements of Internet Information Server, capabilities of the product, and limitations, as well. The knowledge needed here also requires understanding of general networking concepts.

Objective for Planning

- Choose a security strategy for various situations

- Choose an implementation strategy for an Internet site or an intranet site for standalone servers, single-domain environments, and multiple-domain environments.

- Choose the appropriate technology to resolve specified problems.

Installation and Configuration

The Installation and Configuration part of the IIS exam is a substantial component of the exam. You are tested on virtually every possible installation and configuration possibility.

Objectives for Installation and Configuration

- Install IIS

- Configure IIS to support the FTP service

- Configure IIS to support the WWW service

- Configure and save consoles by using Microsoft Management Console

- Verify server settings by accessing the metabase

- Choose the appropriate administration method

- Install and configure Certificate Server

- Install and configure Microsoft SMTP Service

- Install and configure Microsoft NNTP Service

- Customize the installation of Microsoft Site Server Express Analysis Content Analyzer

- Customize the installation of Site Server Express Analysis Report Writer and Usage Import

Configuring and Managing Resource Access

The Configuring and Managing Resource Access component of the Implementing and Supporting Microsoft Internet Information Server 4.0 certification exam concentrates on how to use the various sharing and authentication components of IIS.

Objectives for Configuring and Managing Resource Access

- Create and share directories with appropriate permissions
- Create and share local and remote virtual directories with appropriate permissions
- Create and share virtual servers with appropriate permissions
- Write scripts to manage the FTP service or the WWW service
- Manage a Web site by using Content Analyzer
- Configure Microsoft SMTP Service to host personal mailboxes
- Configure Microsoft NNTP Service to host a newsgroup
- Configure Certificate Server to issue certificates
- Configure Index Server to index a Web site
- Manage MIME types
- Manage the FTP service
- Manage the WWW Service

Integration and Interoperability

The Integration and Interoperability component of the Implementing and Supporting Microsoft Internet Information Server 4.0 certification exam concentrates on configuring IIS to interact with databases.

Objectives for Integration and Interoperability

- Configure IIS to connect to a database
- Configure IIS to integrate with Index Server

Running Applications

The Running Applications component of the Implementing and Supporting Microsoft Internet Information Server 4.0 certification exam looks at scripting on IIS and the options available to do so.

Objectives for Running Applications

- Configure IIS to support server-side scripting
- Configure IIS to run ISAPI applications
- Configure IIS to support ADO associated with the WWW service

Monitoring and Optimization

The Monitoring and Optimization component of the IIS exam looks at how to monitor your site and optimize it for the greatest performance combination attainable.

Objectives for Monitoring and Optimization

- Maintain a log for fine-tuning and auditing purposes
- Monitor performance of various functions by using Performance Monitor
- Analyze performance
- Optimize performance of IIS
- Optimize performance of Index Server
- Optimize performance of Microsoft SMTP Service
- Optimize performance of Microsoft NNTP Service

- Interpret performance data

- Optimize a Web site by using Content Analyzer

Troubleshooting

The Troubleshooting component of the IIS certification exam has eight components running the entire gamut of troubleshooting.

Objectives for Troubleshooting

- Resolve IIS configuration problems

- Resolve security problems

- Resolve resource access problems

- Resolve Index Server query problems

- Resolve setup issues when installing IIS on a Windows NT Server 4.0 computer

- Use a WebMap to find and repair broken links, hyperlink texts, headings, and titles

- Resolve WWW service problems

- Resolve FTP service problems

HARDWARE AND SOFTWARE RECOMMENDED FOR PREPARATION

The *IIS 4 Fast Track* is meant to help you review concepts with which you already have training and hands-on experience. To make the most of the review, you need to have as much background and experience as possible. The best way to do this is to combine studying with working on real networks using the products on which you will be tested. This section gives you a description of the minimum computer requirements you will need to build a solid practice environment.

Computers

The minimum computer requirements to ensure you can study on everything on which you'll be tested is one or more workstations running Windows 95 or NT Workstation, and two or more servers running Windows NT Server, all connected by a network.

Workstations: Windows 95 and Windows NT

- Computer on the Microsoft Hardware Compatibility list
- 486DX 33 MHz
- 16MB of RAM
- 200MB hard disk
- 3.5-inch 1.44MB floppy drive
- VGA video adapter
- VGA monitor
- Mouse or equivalent pointing device
- Two-speed CD-ROM drive
- Network Interface Card (NIC)
- Presence on an existing network, or use of a hub to create a test network
- Microsoft Windows 95 or NT Workstation 4.0

Servers: Windows NT Server

- Two computers on the Microsoft Hardware Compatibility List
- 486DX2 66 MHz
- 32MB of RAM
- 340MB hard disk
- 3.5-inch 1.44MB floppy drive
- VGA video adapter
- VGA monitor

- Mouse or equivalent pointing device

- Two-speed CD-ROM drive

- Network Interface Card (NIC)

- Presence on an existing network, or use of a hub to create a test network

- Microsoft Windows NT Server 4.0

OBJECTIVE REVIEW NOTES

The Objective Review Notes feature of the *Fast Track* series contains a separate section—two to a page—for each subobjective covered in the book. Each subobjective section falls under the main exam objective category, just as you'd expect to find it. It is strongly suggested that you review each subobjective and immediately make note of your knowledge level; then return to the Objective Review Notes section repeatedly and document your progress. Your ultimate goal should be to be able to review only this section and know if you are ready for the exam.

Suggested use:

1. Read the objective. Refer to the part of the book where it's covered. Then ask yourself the following questions:

   - Do you already know this material? Then check "Got it" and make a note of the date.

   - Do you need some brushing up on the objective area? Check "Review it" and make a note of the date. While you're at it, write down the page numbers you just checked, because you'll need to return to that section.

   - Is this material something you're largely unfamiliar with? Check the "Help!" box and write down the date. Now you can get to work.

2. You get the idea. Keep working through the material in this book and in the other study material you probably have. The more you get the material, the quicker you can update and upgrade each objective notes section from "Help!" to "Review it" to "Got it."

3. Cross reference to the materials YOU are using. Most people who take certification exams use more than one resource at a time. Write down the page numbers of where this material is covered in other books you're using, or which software program and file this material is covered on, or which video tape (and counter number) it's on, or whatever you need that works for you.

Think of this as your personal study diary—your documentation of how you beat this exam.

PART II: INSIDE EXAM 70-087

Part II of this book is designed to round out your exam preparation by providing you with chapters that do the following:

- ◆ "Fast Facts Review" is a digest of all "What Is Important to Know" sections from all Part I chapters. Use this chapter to review just before you take the exam: It's all here, in an easily reviewable format.

- ◆ "Insider's Spin on Exam 70-087" grounds you in the particulars for preparing mentally for this examination and for Microsoft testing in general.

- ◆ "Sample Test Questions" provides a full length practice exam that tests you on the actual material covered in Part I. If you mastered the material there, you should be able to pass with flying colors here.

- ◆ "Hotlist of Exam-Critical Concepts" is your resource for cross-checking your tech terms. Although you're probably up to speed on most of this material already, double-check yourself anytime you run across an item you're not 100% certain about; it could make a difference at exam time.

- ◆ "Did You Know?" is the last-day-of-class bonus chapter: A brief touching-upon of peripheral information designed to be helpful and of interest to anyone using this technology to the point that they wish to be certified in its mastery.

WHAT'S IMPORTANT TO KNOW ABOUT EXAM 70-087

MCSE Fast Track: Internet Information Server 4 is written as a study aid for people preparing for Microsoft Certification Exam 70-087. The book is intended to help reinforce and clarify information with which the student is already familiar. This series is not intended to be a single source for exam preparation, but rather a review of information and set of practice tests to help increase the likelihood of success when taking the actual exam.

Part I of this book is designed to help you make the most of your study time by presenting concise summaries of information that you need to understand to succeed on the exam. Each chapter covers a specific exam objective area as outlined by Microsoft:

1   **Planning**

2   **Installation and Configuration**

3   **Configuring and Managing Resource Access**

4   **Integration and Interoperability**

5   **Running Applications**

6   **Monitoring and Optimization**

7   **Troubleshooting**

ABOUT THE EXAM

Exam Number	**70-087**
Minutes	**90***
Questions	**60***
Passing Score	**666***
Single Answer Questions:	Yes
Multiple Answer with Correct Number Given	Yes
Multiple Answer Without Correct Number Given	**Minimal**
Ranking Order	Yes
Choices of A–D	Yes
Choices of A–E	No
Objective Categories	7

Note: These exam criteria will no longer apply when this exam goes to an adaptive format.

▶ Choose a security strategy for various situations. Security considerations include:
  - Controlling anonymous access
  - Controlling access to known users and groups
  - Controlling access by host or network
  - Configuring SSL to provide encryption and authentication schemes
  - Identifying the appropriate balance between security requirements and performance requirements

▶ Choose an implementation strategy for an Internet site or an intranet site for standalone servers, single-domain environments, and multiple-domain environments. Tasks include:
  - Resolving host header name issues by using a HOSTS file, DNS, or both
  - Choosing the appropriate operating system on which to install IIS

▶ Choose the appropriate technology to resolve specified problems. Technology options include:
  - WWW service
  - FTP Service
  - Microsoft Transaction Server
  - Microsoft SMTP Service
  - Microsoft NNTP Service
  - Microsoft Index Server
  - Microsoft Certificate Server

CHAPTER 1

Planning

CHOOSING A SECURITY STRATEGY

Microsoft Internet Information Server (IIS) 4.0 incorporates a number of security features into its service, as well as builds on Windows NT 4.0's security. When implementing IIS, there are several factors to consider in terms of security, and the following sections examine these considerations.

Controlling Anonymous Access

Anonymous access enables clients to access your servers (FTP or WWW) without giving a name, or using the name "anonymous." Traditionally, WWW access has been completely anonymous, and FTP has been the same, with users using the userID of "anonymous." When finished, they can then log into your site by using their email address as their password.

IIS uses the default IUSR_*computername* account for all anonymous logons. This account, like all other user accounts, appears in the User Manager for Domains utility (shown in Figure 1.1) and can be administered from there.

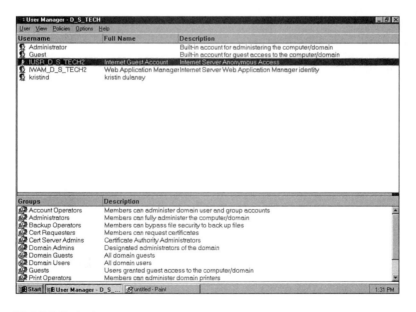

FIGURE 1.1
The anonymous user account can be administered from User Manager for Domains.

Permissions set up for this account determine an anonymous user's privileges. The default properties are shown in Figure 1.2, including the fact that the user cannot change the password, and the password does not expire.

Anonymous FTP

On the Accounts Security tab of the FTP Service Properties sheet, you can configure the following options:

+ **Allow Anonymous Connections.** Select this for anonymous connections.

+ **Username.** Displays the IUSR_*computername* name as set up by IIS in the Windows NT User Manager for Domains and in the Internet Service Manager.

+ **Password.** A randomly generated password was created by User Manger for Domains and Internet Service Manager. You must have a password here; no blanks are allowed. If you change this password, make sure it matches the one in the User Manager for Domains and Internet Service Manager for this user.

+ **Allow only anonymous connections.** Click this option to limit access to your FTP server to only those who log on as anonymous. This restricts users from logging on with an account that has administrative rights. New to IIS 4.0, Enable Automatic Password Synchronization has been added as an option to eliminate accidental password inconsistencies between IIS 4 and User Manager.

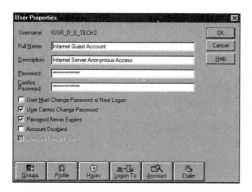

FIGURE 1.2
The default anonymous user account properties.

◆ **Administrator.** Select those accounts who are allowed to administer this virtual FTP site. To administer a virtual FTP site, users must first be a member of the Administrative group under Windows NT. Click the Add button to add a user account to this list. Remove an account by selecting the account and clicking Remove.

Anonymous WWW

IIS 4.0 can be set up to verify the identity of clients who access your Web site. On public Web sites on which non-critical or public domain information and applications are available, authentication of users connecting to your Web site may not be important. However, if you have secure data or want to restrict Web access to specific clients, logon and authentication requirements become very important.

Use the following steps to set authentication and logon requirements:

1. Open Internet Service Manager.

2. Right-click a Web site, file (NTFS systems only), or directory you want to configure. You can still implement security on files that are located on FAT partitions. The only parameters that are available are Read and Write. If the files reside on an NTFS partition, the most restrictive takes precedence.

3. Click Properties. The property sheet for that item will appear, as shown in Figure 1.3.

FIGURE 1.3
The properties for a Web site are available through IIS.

4. Click the Directory Security tab (or File Security if you want to set file-specific properties).

5. Click the Edit button under Anonymous Access and Authentication Control. The Authentication Methods dialog box appears, as shown in Figure 1.4.

6. Select an authentication method from the following options:

- ◆ **Allow Anonymous Access.** Enables clients to connect to your Web site without requiring a username or password. Click the Edit button to select the Windows NT user account used to access your computer. The default account IUSR_*computer-name* is used. This account is granted Log on Locally user rights by default and is necessary for anonymous logon access to your Web site. Click OK to return to the Authentication Methods dialog box.

- ◆ **Basic Authentication.** Use this method if you do not specify anonymous access and you want a client connecting to your Web site to enter a valid Windows NT username and password to log on. This sends a password in clear text format with the passwords being transmitted in an unencrypted format. Click the Edit button to specify a default logon domain for users who do not explicitly name a domain.

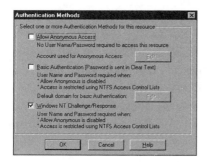

FIGURE 1.4
The authentication methods can be defined for each Web site.

♦ **Windows NT Challenge/Response.** This setting is used if you want the Windows NT Challenge/Response feature to authenticate the client attempting to connect to your Web site. The only Web browsers that support this feature include Internet Explorer 2.0 and later. During the challenge/response procedure, cryptographic information is exchanged between the client and server to authenticate the user.

7. Click OK.

Normally, you want anonymous WWW access at most sites. This is not the case, however, if you are dealing with sensitive data. SSL provides for data confidentiality by encrypting the data that is transmitted. In that situation, you can prevent the use of anonymous access by requiring IIS to authenticate users. Authentication can be done on the basis of known users and groups, by host or network, or by Secure Socket Layer authentication. SSL itself, does not provide the authentication unless client-side certificates are required.

Authentication of users will take place only if you have disabled anonymous access, or anonymous access fails because there is not an anonymous account with appropriate permissions in NTFS.

Controlling Access to Known Users and Groups

As opposed to the anonymous model discussed above, you can use NTFS (NT File System) permissions to limit access to your site to a defined set of users or groups. In this situation, all users must have a Windows NT account that is valid, and they must provide the user ID and password to establish the connection. Once connected, the permissions set for the user govern what they can and cannot access.

NTFS permissions can be broken into five categories:

♦ **Change.** Assigns Read (R), Execute (X), Write (W), and Delete (D) permissions.

♦ **Full Control.** Assigns R, X, W, and D permissions. This also includes the ability to Change Permissions and Take Ownership.

- **No Access.** The No Access overrides all other permissions. It still allows users to connect, but nothing shows up except the message `You do not have permission to access this directory.`

- **Read.** Assigns only R and X permissions.

- **Special Access.** Whatever you define.

As with all Windows NT permissions, user and group permissions accumulate, with the exception of No Access, which instantly overrides all other permissions.

Controlling Access by Host or Network

In addition to limiting access to your site on the basis of users or groups, you can also limit it based on the host or network that the access is coming from. There are two models you can operate under. The first is where you select a group of networks or hosts and grant them access. In so doing, you are saying that only they can come in, while everyone else is denied access.

The other model is to select a group of networks or hosts and deny them access. In so doing, you are saying that this group is not allowed access, while everyone else is. The solution to your situation is dependent on your individual site and needs.

To grant access to only a few, do the following:

1. Start Internet Service Manager, select the Web site (or file, or directory), and open the properties.

2. Choose either Directory Security or File Security, based on which one you want to assign access for, as shown in Figure 1.5.

3. Click Edit under IP Address and Domain Name Restrictions.

4. Select Denied Access from the IP Address and Domain Name Restrictions dialog box.

5. Click Add.

6. Select either Single Computer, Group of Computers, or Domain Name from the Grant Access On dialog box, shown in Figure 1.6.

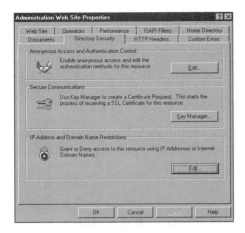

FIGURE 1.5
The Directory Security property choices for the Web site.

FIGURE 1.6
The three methods of denying access to a Web site.

7. Type in the IP address of those you are allowing access, or click the DNS Lookup button to browse for them by name.

8. Click OK twice.

If you select Group of Computers, you must also specify the subnet value indicating the number of computers allowed (or conversely, denied) access.

The following AT A GLANCE box summarizes the available subnet mask values that can be created by dividing the IP address between the host and the subnet. For a more thorough discussion of this topic, see *MCSE Fast Track: TCP/IP* by New Riders Publishing.

At A Glance: Valid Subnet Addresses

Last Digits of Subnet Address	Number of Addresses in Range
192	64
224	32
240	16
248	8
252	4
254	2
255	1 (not used)

Configuring SSL

Secure Sockets Layer (SSL) enables you to protect communications over a network whether that network is an intranet or the Internet. It does so by establishing a private (and encrypted) communication link between the user and the server.

To enable SSL on your server, do the following steps:

1. Start Internet Service Manager and click the Key Manager icon. The Key Manager utility appears, as shown in Figure 1.7.

2. Use Key Manager to generate a certificate request file by choosing Create New Key.

3. Submit the request for a certificate to an online authority and obtain its approval (which can take between days and months).

4. Save the certificate, which is returned as an ASCII file.

5. Start Internet Service Manager once more and click Key Manager. Select the key from the window and choose Install Key Certificate.

6. Select a Web site in Internet Service Manager and open the properties.

7. Go to Advanced under Web Site Identification.

8. Assign the Web site IP address to port 443 under the Multiple SSL identities of this Web Site dialog box.

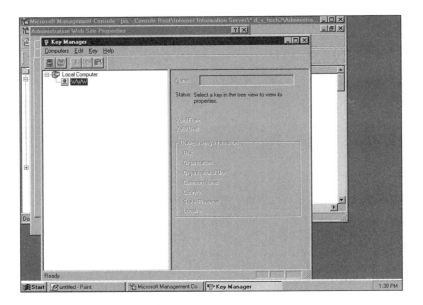

FIGURE 1.7
The Key Manager utility.

9. Click Edit on the Secure Communications option of the property sheet. This opens the Secure Communications dialog box.

10. On the Secure Communications dialog box, set the Web server to require a secure channel and enable the Web server's SSL client certificate authentication.

As an interesting aside, SSL can be used not only to authenticate specific users, but also the anonymous user. If SSL is enabled and a user attempts anonymous access, the Web server will look for a valid certificate on the client and reject those lacking such.

Identifying the Appropriate Balance Between Security and Performance Requirements

In the absence of security, users can access resources without any difficulties. In the presence of absolute security, users cannot access resources at all. Somewhere between the two ends of the extreme lies the security-to-usability equilibrium you are striving for. Determining where that equilibrium lies at each site is the responsibility of the administrator.

Common sense plays a large part in the decision on how much security to implement. For example, security should be tighter at any financial institution, or site conducting financial transactions, than at a user's home page. Likewise, site security should be tighter at any site involving medical or employment information than one containing sports scores.

For an intranet, you should consider creating a group of users who need to access your documents, and assigning the Log on Locally right to the group. Use Windows NT Challenge/Response for authentication, and make certain that only the selected group has the permissions to read and access the documents.

For a public Web site, consider using Microsoft Certificate Server in combination with Secure Sockets Layer (SSL).

Understanding Implementation Strategies

When implementing IIS, there are several factors to consider:

- The environment
- The method of host name resolution
- The operating system

In the following paragraphs, we will concentrate on the environment issues. The following sections examine the host name issues and operating system possibilities.

There are three possibilities for IIS environments in the Windows NT world: on a standalone server, in a single-domain environment, and in a multiple-domain environment.

On a standalone server, it is important that IIS be able to interact with the LAN, WAN, or other network architecture that you are seeking. Confining IIS to a standalone server adds a level of security in that users who penetrate the security of the server are able to access only that server and nothing more.

In a single-domain environment, IIS is often installed on the Primary Domain Controller. In so doing, IIS is able to capitalize on the security of the PDC and user/resource authentication there. Depending on the network and load, however, it can be more beneficial to place IIS on an NT Server that has been installed as a Server Role instead of a Domain Controller. This allows the server to be a member of the Domain, for security, while not taxing it with authentication duties.

> **NOTE**   Microsoft's recommendation is that Domain Controllers should never serve any purpose other than authentication. What takes place in the real world, however, is often a different story.

In a multiple-domain environment, it is important that IIS be accessible to all the domains. Bandwidth becomes extremely important as the server faces the limitations of the "wire." Thought should be given to using the best (fastest) Network Interface Card possible with an ample amount of RAM and a fast processor to service all the traffic the IIS server will need to service. As a general rule, the entire IO subsystem (including the hard drive controller, hard drive, and NIC) is the most critical component in the quest for speed.

Resolving Host Name Issues with HOSTS or DNS

There are two methods of resolving host names in a Windows NT environment:

- With static HOSTS files
- With DNS

TCP/IP issues and knowledge you *must* carry over from the TCP/IP exam to this one include the IP classes and default subnet mask values shown in the following AT A GLANCE.

At A Glance: TCP/IP Classes

Class	Address	Number of Hosts Available	Default Subnet Mask
A	01-126	16,777,214	255.0.0.0
B	128-191	65,534	255.255.0.0
C	192-223	254	255.255.255.0

Choosing an Appropriate Operating System

There are three operating systems that IIS 4.0 will run on: Windows NT Server, Windows NT Workstation, and Windows 95.

Windows 95 should not be considered a practical choice for a production environment, as it—in and of itself—is not a server operating system. Windows 95 is limited to only one connection at a time, and has no built-in method of true, secure, user authentication. Windows 95, however, is an excellent platform for a mobile development workforce to use on laptops while fine-tuning IIS applications that aren't yet live.

Windows NT Workstation 4.0 includes Peer Web Services, a limited version of IIS 2.0. Windows NT Workstation can be used with IIS for a very small Intranet implementation. The number of concurrent connections Workstation can support is limited to 10, and that makes the product less than minimal for an Internet Server service. Like Windows 95, it is ideal for a laptop operating system.

Windows NT Server 4.0 supports an unlimited number of concurrent connections, up to 256 phone connections (RAS), and is fine-tuned for a production server environment. As such, there is no better operating system on which to run IIS, and this should be the one used in all production Internet environments.

CHOOSING APPROPRIATE TECHNOLOGIES

There are a number of servers and services that come with the basic Internet Information Server 4.0 product. Many of these have been with IIS since version 2.0 or before, while several are new to this release. Choosing the right server or service to add can only be accomplished by understanding the purpose behind each.

WWW

Often synonymously used for the Internet, the World Wide Web is but one component of it. The Internet has been in existence for years, but never gained fame with the masses until the World Wide Web was created to place a graphical service on it.

Use the World Wide Web if you want to include HTML (Hypertext Markup Language) documents on your site, as illustrated in Figure 1.8, and allow remote clients and browsers to reach them.

FTP

An FTP (File Transport Protocol) server provides clients attaching to your server the capability of transmitting files to and from the server, as illustrated in Figure 1.9.

Although FTP is one of the oldest Internet services, it is still the fastest and one of the most popular ways to transfer files over the Internet.

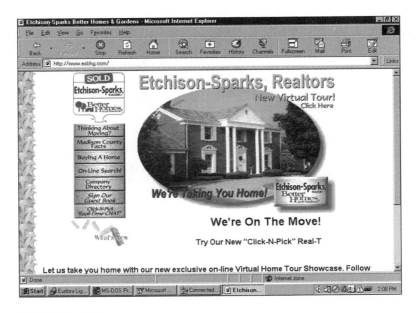

FIGURE 1.8
An Example of a WWW site.

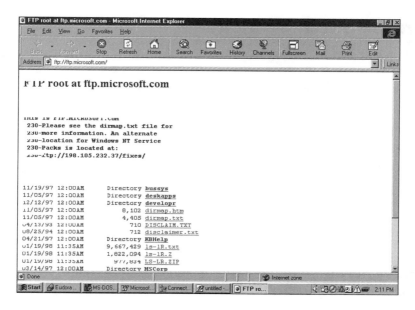

FIGURE 1.9
An example of an FTP site.

Microsoft Transaction Server

Microsoft Transaction Server (MTS) is a transaction processing system for managing and developing server applications. It enables you to keep track of transactions that occur on the server.

Microsoft SMTP Service

Microsoft SMTP Service uses the Simple Mail Transfer Protocol to send and receive email using TCP port 25 for operations. Once installed, it can be managed and administered through Internet Service Manager or Internet Service Manager for SMTP Service. The two function almost identically, with the difference being that the latter enables you to administer SMTP through HTML, whereas the former requires administration from the server.

Microsoft NNTP Service

The Microsoft NNTP service supports the Network News Transport Protocol and enables clients to access newsgroups. You can reach and interact with existing newsgroups in your organization, or create new ones.

Microsoft NNTP supports MIME, HTML, GIF, and JPEG. Like SMTP, once installed it can be managed and administered through Internet Service Manager or Internet Service Manager for SMTP Service.

Microsoft Index Server

Microsoft Index Server indexes Web content at your Internet or intranet site to allow clients to quickly find information through queries. It includes a query engine that can find the results, and then has the ability to format the results to meet specifications you define.

Index Server can work with HTML documents as well as Excel and Word documents.

Microsoft Certificate Server

Microsoft Certificate Server enables you to increase the security of your site by issuing certificates (digital identifiers) that use public-key encryption. This allows you to verify that you have secure communication across the network, whether that network be an intranet or the Internet. The server certificates are issued from a third-party organization and contain information about the organization and the public key.

With public-key encryption, there are actually two keys involved, forming a key pair. The first is the public key, which is a known value and the one used to establish a secure HTTP connection. The second key is a private key, known only by the user. The two are mathematical opposites of each other, used to negotiate a secure TCP/IP connection.

When the connection is established, a session key (typically 40 bits in length) is used between the server and client to encrypt and decrypt the transmissions.

Certificate Server is an integral component of the Microsoft Internet Security Framework (ISF) model. Said integration means that Windows NT users and groups can be mapped to certificates and the users still receive the benefit of a single logon to the network.

Requests for certificates come into Microsoft Certificate Server across HTTP, email, or as Remote Procedure Calls. Every request is verified against a policy before being responded to in X.509 format (used for authentication with the SSL protocol). Different policies can be in place for different groups of users, and policy modules can be written in Microsoft Visual Basic, C++, or Java.

The browsers that request the certificates must be Microsoft Internet Explorer 3.0 or later or Netscape Navigator 3.0 or later.

WHAT IS IMPORTANT TO KNOW

The following bullets summarize the chapter and accentuate the key concepts to memorize for the exam:

- IIS can be installed on a standalone machine, or in almost any other configuration.

- IIS can be installed on a workstation, or server, but the workstation should only be used as a test environment, and is not suitable for most purposes.

- For the WWW service, available authentication methods are:

  - **Allow Anonymous Access**. Enables clients to connect to your Web site without requiring a username or password by using the default account of IUSR_*computername*.

  - **Basic Authentication**. This method is used if you do not specify anonymous access and you want a client connecting to your Web site to enter a valid Windows NT username and password to log on. This sends a password in clear text format with the passwords being transmitted in an unencrypted format.

  - **Windows NT Challenge/Response**. This setting is used if you want the Windows NT Challenge/Response feature to authenticate the client attempting to connect to your Web site. The only Web browsers that support this feature include Internet Explorer 2.0 and later. During the challenge/response procedure, cryptographic information is exchanged between the client and server to authenticate the user.

- For the FTP service, available authentication methods include the ability to specify that anonymous connections are allowed, only anonymous connections are allowed, or the administrator can configure user and group accounts.

- You cannot specify that only anonymous connections are allowed until you have first allowed anonymous connections.

- The basics of TCP/IP address class are recapped in the following table:

Class	Address	Number of Hosts Available	Default Subnet Mask
A	01-126	16,777,214	255.0.0.0
B	128-191	65,534	255.255.0.0
C	192-223	254	255.255.255.0

- The WINS service is used for dynamic resolution of NetBIOS names to IP addresses, whereas DNS is used for the resolution of host names to

IP addresses. The static version of each is the LMHOSTS and HOSTS files, respectively.

◆ Secure Sockets Layer (SSL) enables you to protect communications over a network whether that network be an intranet or the Internet. It does so by establishing a private (and encrypted) communication link between the user and the server. SSL can be used not only to authenticate specific users, but also the anonymous user. If SSL is enabled and a user attempts anonymous access, the Web server will look for a valid certificate on the client and reject those lacking such. To use SSL, you must obtain a digital certificate from an authentication authority and use Key Manager to generate keys. SSL URLs begin with https:// instead of http://

◆ For the exam, memorize the table of subnets and the number of hosts that each subnet makes available on a C level network:

Last Digits of Subnet Address	Number of Addresses in Range
192	64
224	32
240	16
248	8
252	4
254	2
255	1 (not used)

▶ Install IIS. Tasks include:
- Configuring a Microsoft Windows NT Server 4.0 computer for the installation of IIS
- Identifying differences to a Windows NT Server 4.0 computer made by the installation of IIS

▶ Configure IIS to support the FTP service. Tasks include:
- Setting bandwidth and user connections
- Setting user logon requirements and authentication requirements
- Modifying port settings
- Setting directory listing style
- Configuring virtual directories and servers

▶ Configure IIS to support the WWW service
- Setting bandwidth and user connections
- Setting user logon requirements and authentication requirements
- Modifying port settings
- Setting default pages
- Setting HTTP 1.1 host header names to host multiple Web sites
- Enabling HTTP Keep-Alives

▶ Configure and save consoles by using Microsoft Management Console

▶ Verify server settings by accessing the metabase

▶ continues…

CHAPTER 2

Installation and Configuration

OBJECTIVES continued

▶ Choose the appropriate administration method

▶ Install and configure Certificate Server

▶ Install and configure Microsoft SMTP Service

▶ Install and configure Microsoft NNTP Service

▶ Customize the installation of Microsoft Site Server Express Content Analyzer

▶ Customize the installation of Microsoft Site Server Express Usage Import and Report Writer

INSTALLING **IIS**

Microsoft Internet Information Server (IIS) 4.0 is the newest Internet and Web server designed to run under Windows NT Server 4.0. Setting up and configuring IIS is the first step in setting up an Internet or intranet site.

At A Glance: IIS Ports

IIS Service	Default Port Assignment
FTP	21
SMTP	25
WWW	80
NNTP	119
SSL	443
NNTP with SSL	563

IIS 4 includes the following features:

- SMTP Mail Server
- Microsoft Management Console
- NNTP News Server
- Script Debugger
- Usage Analyst
- Web Publishing Wizard
- Windows Scripting Host
- FrontPage Server Administrator

After you install IIS 4.0, you can add Hypertext Markup Language (HTML) files to your server for users to connect to and view.

Configuring a Microsoft Windows NT Server 4.0 Computer For the Installation of IIS

IIS 4.0 is available only as part of the Windows NT 4.0 Option Pack. Currently, IIS 4 is available on CD-ROM from Microsoft or as a large download from Microsoft's Web site. You can download it as part of the Windows NT 4.0 Option Pack from Microsoft at http://www.microsoft.com/downtrial/optionpack.asp. You also can order an Option Pack CD-ROM from Microsoft from the same site. With this download, you're provided with IIS 4, Microsoft Site Server Express 2.0, Transaction Server 2.0, Microsoft Message Queue Server 1.0, Certificate Server 1.0, Index Server Express, Internet Explorer 4.0, remote-access services for virtual networking, and Windows NT Service Pack 3.

Before you set up IIS 4, your system must meet or exceed the hardware requirements summarized in Tables 2.1 and 2.2. Table 2.1 shows requirements for a system running an Intel x86 processor. Table 2.2 lists requirements for a system running a DEC Alpha processor.

TABLE 2.1

IIS 4 HARDWARE REQUIREMENTS FOR AN INTEL SYSTEM

Hardware Device	Requirements
CPU	Minimum of a 50 MHz (90 MHz recommended) 486 DX processor. For bettor performance, you need a Pentium 133 or higher processor.
Hard disk space	Minimum of 50MB, but it is recommended you have at least 200MB. This does not include storage needed for files you plan to distribute via IIS.
Memory	Minimum of 16MB. For a Web site on which you will store multimedia files or expect a great deal of traffic, 32–64MB is the recommended minimum.
Monitor	Super VGA monitor with 800 × 600 resolution.

TABLE 2.2

IIS 4 HARDWARE REQUIREMENTS FOR AN ALPHA SYSTEM

Hardware Device	Requirements
CPU	Minimum of 150 MHz processor (200 MHz recommended).
Hard disk space	Minimum of 50MB, but you should allocate up to 200MB for best performance.
Memory	Minimum of 48MB. For better performance, have at least 64MB.
Monitor	Super VGA monitor with 800 × 600 resolution.

Before you install IIS 4.0, remove any installations of a previous version of IIS. You'll also need to disable other versions of FTP, Gopher, or World Wide Web services you have installed under Windows NT Server 4.0. This includes the Windows Academic Centre (EMWAC) service included with the Windows NT Resource Kit.

You also should have the following software installed:

♦ Windows NT Server 4.0

♦ Service Pack 3 for Windows NT Server 4.0

♦ Internet Explorer (4.01 or later).

You also must be logged on to the Windows NT Server computer with Administrator privileges.

Another consideration before installing IIS 4 is to install TCP/IP (Transmission Control Protocol/Internet Protocol) on your Windows NT 4.0 computer. TCP/IP is used to provide Internet connectivity to retrieve data from the Internet, as well as a hosting computer on the Internet.

For systems in which file-level security is needed, configure Windows NT Server with the NT File System (NTFS). NTFS enables you to limit access to files and directories. Systems running FAT do not allow you to limit access at the file level, only the directory level. You can still implement security at the file level, but the only restrictions that you can place are Read, Write, or neither. This security is handled through the IIS services.

Finally, you should consider installing DHCP (Dynamic Host Configuration Protocol) if you plan to run IIS 4 on an intranet. DHCP automatically assigns IP (Internet Protocol) addresses to computers connecting to the server that are set up to use DHCP. For systems connecting to the Internet, you need to acquire a TCP/IP address from the InterNIC or from an Internet Service Provider (ISP).

Installing IIS 4.0

After you set up Windows NT Server 4.0 to receive IIS 4.0, you're ready to start the IIS 4.0 setup program. Make sure you are connected to the Internet or to your intranet before installing IIS.

To start IIS 4.0 setup, insert the Option Pack CD-ROM and locate the Setup icon in Explorer. Double-click the Setup icon. Or, if you downloaded IIS 4.0 from the Internet, double-click the setup file.

NOTE

IIS 4.0 relies on Internet Explorer 4.01 for many of its management and configuration tasks. If you do not already have IE 4 installed, you'll be prompted to install it when you start the IIS 4.0 setup routine. Be sure to click Yes if prompted to install IE 4. Windows NT will need to shut down and restart before continuing with the IIS installation.

Next, follow these steps:

1. Click Next on the Welcome to the Windows NT 4.0 Option Pack Setup dialog box. The End User License Agreement screen appears.

2. Click Accept.

3. Click Custom. A dialog box with components will appear. You also can click Minimum or Typical, but these steps assume you want to have control over the components that are installed.

4. Click the component you want to install. If you want to change the specific options (called subcomponents) that install with the components, click the Show Subcomponents button. This displays a

dialog box with the specific options that fall under a component heading. Selected components and subcomponents have check marks next to them.

Specific components and their subcomponents are listed in Table 2.3.

TABLE 2.3

IIS 4.0 SETUP OPTIONS

Component	Subcomponents	Description
Certificate Server	Certificate Server Certificate Authority	Enables you to create Certificate Authority on the IIS server to issue digital certificates to users accessing your Web.
	Certificate Server Documentation	Documents to help you install and configure Certificate Authorities.
	Certificate Server Web Client	Enables you to post Web pages on your server to submit requests and retrieve certificates from a Certificate Authority.
FrontPage 98 Server Extensions	FrontPage Server Extensions files	Enables you to author Web pages and administer Web sites using Microsoft FrontPage and Visual InterDev.
Visual InterDev RAD	Visual InterDev RAD Remote Deployment Support	Enables you to deploy applications remotely on the Web server.
Internet Information Server (IIS)	Common Program Files	Files used by several IIS components.
	Documentation	Product documentation for IIS.
	File Transfer Protocol (FTP) Server	Provides FTP support to set up an FTP site to allow users to upload and download files from your site.
	Internet News Server	Installs the Microsoft Internet News Server for NNTP news.

continues

TABLE 2.3 continued

Component	Subcomponents	Description
	Internet Service Manager	Provides a snap-in for the Microsoft Management Console (MMC) to administer IIS.
	Internet Service Manager (HTML)	Provides an HTML-based administrative tool for IIS. You use IE 4 with this manager to administer IIS.
	SMTP Server	Installs the SMTP (Simple Mail Transfer Protocol) Server for email.
	World Wide Web samples	Installs sample IIS Web sites and other samples.
	World Wide Web Server	Installs the Web server so clients can access your Web site.
Microsoft Data Access Components 1.5 (MDAC, ADO, ODBC, and OLE) (ADO) 1.5	ActiveX Data Objects	Installs the ActiveX Data Objects and other OLE DB and ODBC files.
	Data Sources	Installs the drivers and providers to access common data sources, including Jet and Access (ODBC), Oracle, and SQL Server data sources.
	Remote Data Service 1.5 (RDS/ADC)	Installs Remote Data Service. Click the Show Subcomponents button to see options for this subcomponent.
Microsoft Index Server	Index Server System Files	Installs the files for the Index Server system.
	Language Resources	Installs Index Server language resources. Click the Show Subcomponents button to see a list of these languages. US English Language is the default setting.
	Online Documentation	Installs Index Server documentation.

Component	*Subcomponents*	*Description*
	Sample Files	Installs sample files on how to use the Index Server.
Microsoft Message Queue (MSMQ)	Administration Guide	Installs the MSMQ Administration Guide.
	Administration Tools	Enables you to control and monitor your message queuing enterprise.
	Microsoft Message Queue Server	Installs the required MSMQ files.
	Software Development Kit	Installs the MSMQ SDK for creating MSMQ applications with C or C++ APIs, or with ActiveX components.
Microsoft Script Debugger	Microsoft Script Debugger	Installs the Microsoft Script Debugger to debug Active Server Pages scripts and applications.
Microsoft Site Server Express 2.0	Analysis—Content	Enables you to analyze your site with content, site visualization, link management, and reporting tool.
	Analysis—Usage	Enables you to analyze your site usage.
	Publishing— Posting Acceptor 1.01	Lets IIS receive files uploaded to it using the HTTP POST protocol.
	Publishing—Web Publishing Wizard 1.52	Automatically uploads new or revised content to Web servers.
Internet Connection Services for RAS (Remote Access Services)	Connection Manager Administration Kit	Sets up dial-up profiles in Connection Manager.
	Connection Point Services	Provides administration and services to phonebooks.
	Internet Authentication Services	Installs the Internet Authentication Service.

continues

TABLE 2.3 continued

Component	Subcomponents	Description
	Product Documentation	Installs documentation for Remote Access Services.
Transaction Server	Microsoft Management Console	Installs MMC, which is an interface for systems management applications.
	Transaction Server (MTS) Core Components	Installs MTS files.
	Transaction Server Core Documentation	Installs MTS product documentation.
	Transaction Server Deployment	Installs headers, libraries, and samples to help you create transaction components.
Windows Scripting Host	Windows Scripting Host Files	Installs executable files for the Windows Scripting Host.

The following steps assume all components and subcomponents are selected. Depending on your choices, you may not see all the dialog boxes shown in these steps.

5. Click Next. A dialog box showing the default publishing folders appears. The following list summarizes these folders:

- Web services are installed in the C:\Inetpub\wwwroot folder.

- FTP services are installed in the C:\Inetpub\ftproot folder.

- Applications are installed in the C:\Program Files folder.

You can change any of these default folders by typing over them or clicking the Browse button next to them.

6. Click Next. The Transaction Server dialog box displays. The MTS Install Folder field shows where Transaction Server will be installed. By default, this folder is named C:\MTS. You can change this folder if you want.

7. Click Next. A dialog box to set remote administration features displays. You can choose to administer IIS from a Local account, in which no other account information is needed, or from a Remote account on another machine, which requires the Administrator Account name and its password. You can click the Browse button to locate the Administrator Account.

8. Click Next. The Index Server dialog box displays the default folder for the index. This default directory is C:\Inetpub. You can change this folder if you like.

9. Click Next. The Mail Server dialog box displays the default folder for the mailroot directory. Other folders (mail queue, mailbox, and badmail) will be created under this folder. The default for this folder is C:\Inetpub\Mailroot.

10. Click Next. The News Server dialog box displays the default folder for the nntpfile directory. Articles and data files used by the news server will be stored under this folder. The default for this folder is C:\Inetpub\nntpfile.

11. Click Next. Select from one of the following types of MSMQ servers:

- **Primary Enterprise Controller (PEC).** Installs only one PEC on the network and contains the master copy of the MSMQ Information Store. This PEC will act as the Primary Site Controller for one site. You must have SQL Server installed to choose this option.

- **Primary Site Controller (PSC).** Installs one PSC for each site, which is a physical set of computers communicating with each other, usually paralleling the physical location of the computers. You must have SQL Server installed to choose this option.

- **Backup Site Controller (BSC).** BSCs provide a backup of the PSC in case the PSC fails. You must have SQL Server installed to choose this option.

- **Routing Server.** Provides routing services, remote message store, and store-and-forward services. These servers are spread across the network to allow messages to reach a target queue via different paths. Each PEC, PSC, and BSC also acts as a Routing Server.

12. Click Next. The Microsoft Certificate Server Setup - Introduction dialog box displays. This wizard shows how to create a new Certificate Authority.

13. Click Next. On the Certificate Server - Choose Storage Location dialog box, enter the location to store configuration files and certificate files. Unless the Windows NT domain controller is available for use, enter a shared folder.

14. Click Next. On the Choose Key Storage Location dialog box, enter the names you want for the System Store and Container for your keys.

15. Click Next. On the Choose Database Location dialog box, you are shown the default folder in which the certificate information will be stored.

16. Click Next. Fill in your identification information, including name, state, country, locality, and other items.

17. Click Next. The Choose CSP and Hashing dialog box shows the Cryptographic Services Providers (CSP) you can select. You also can choose the hash algorithms from the Hash list.

18. Click Next. The Choose Certificate Output File Names dialog box shows the signature and key exchange certificate names. You can change these if necessary; however, the default names should suffice for most installations.

19. Click Next. You can enter a comment to identify the certificate later.

20. Click Next. Setup now completes the installation process and installs the IIS files onto your hard disk. This process may take a long time to complete.

21. Click Finish when all the files are installed to your system.

22. Click Yes when prompted to restart your computer.

After the restart, you will have successfully installed the components. The following section will look at the changes that were actually made to your system as a result of the installation.

Identifying Changes To a Windows NT Server 4.0 Computer Made by the Installation of IIS

When you install IIS 4, your Windows NT Server 4.0 computer will include some new components. These changes include the following:

+ Microsoft Management Console (MMC) is the host for the Internet Service Manager. Internet Service Manager is IIS's administrative program.

+ Registry changes can be viewed by selecting Start, Programs, Windows NT 4.0 Option Pack, Microsoft Site Server Express 2.0, Documentation. Expand the Microsoft Internet Information Server option and click Administrator's Reference in the left pane (see Figure 2.1), and then click Registry. Click the topic you want to read, such as WWW Service Registry Entries.

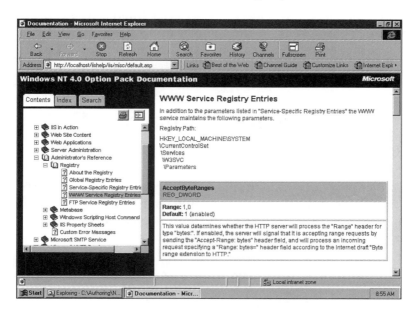

FIGURE 2.1
You can view the different Registry changes from the Windows NT 4.0 Option Pack Documentation.

◆ New services include the FTP Publishing Service, IIS Administration Service, Content Index, and World Wide Web Publishing Service.

NOTE

The three services added during IIS 4 installation—FTP Publishing Service, IIS Administration Service, and World Wide Web Publishing Service—are set to start when you start Windows NT Server. You can change the default settings for each service from the Services dialog box.

◆ User Manager for Domains lists a new username in the list of user accounts. This username is IUSR_*computername* and allows anonymous access to Internet services on your computer.

◆ Performance Monitor can now be used to track several IIS services, including Content Index, Content Index Filter, FTP Service, HTTP Content Index, HTTP Service, and Internet Information Services Global. Some of the more than 75 counters added to Performance Monitor enable you to track connections, bytes transferred, and cache information.

CONFIGURING IIS TO SUPPORT THE FTP SERVICE

An FTP server provides clients attaching to your server the capability of transmitting files to and from the server. Although FTP is one of the oldest Internet services, it is still one of the most popular ways to transfer files over the Internet.

Before your go live with your IIS 4 server, you may want to configure some of the settings relating to FTP. These include:

◆ Setting Bandwidth and User Connections

◆ Setting User Logon Requirements and Authentication Requirements

◆ Modifying Port Settings

◆ Setting Directory Listing Style

◆ Configuring Virtual Directories and Servers

Setting Bandwidth and User Connections is discussed in a later section of this chapter, and the other bullets are discussed in detail in the following sections.

Setting User Logon Requirements and Authentication Requirements

Chapter 1, "Planning," discussed this topic under the headings "Controlling Anonymous Access" and "Anonymous FTP" as they pertained to that portion of the exam. The topics are also considered relevant by Microsoft for the Installation portion of the test, and much of this material will seem familiar from having already seen it once.

In brief, for clients to access your FTP server, you need to set up user logon and authentication requirements—this can be as simple as allowing anonymous connections. With anonymous access, users with the actual name "anonymous" can log into your site using their email address as their password.

By default, IUSR_*computername* is the account used for all anonymous logons.

Modifying Port Settings

Port settings are used by clients to connect to your FTP site. By default, the FTP server is set up with a port setting of 21. You can change this setting to a unique TCP port number, but you must announce this setting to all clients who want to access your server.

Follow these steps to change the port number:

1. Choose the following: Start, Programs, Windows NT 4.0 Option Pack, Microsoft Internet Information Server, Internet Service Manager.

2. Expand the Internet Information Server folder.

3. Expand the server in which you want to modify the port value (see Figure 2.2).

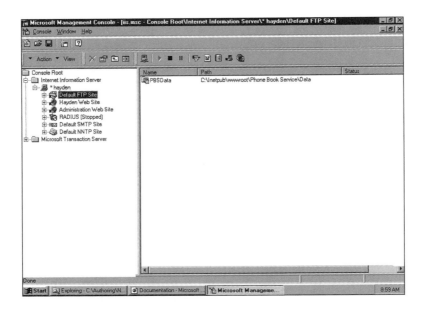

FIGURE 2.2
The Microsoft Management Console provides access to the Internet Service Manager to Administer your FTP Site.

4. Right-click the Default FTP Site entry. Your FTP site may be named something different.

5. Click Properties. The Default FTP Site Properties sheet displays (see Figure 2.3).

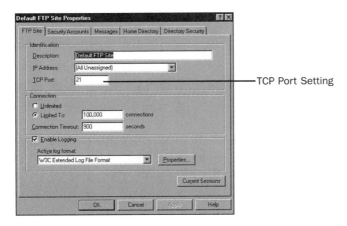

TCP Port Setting

FIGURE 2.3
Use the FTP Site Properties sheet to change the port setting.

6. Change the TCP Port value to a new setting.

7. Click OK.

It is not necessary to restart Windows NT at this point. These settings take effect immediately. The FTP server service does not even need to be stopped and then restarted.

Setting Directory Listing Style

A directory listing style is the way in which your server will display a directory listing. Because Windows NT Server uses a listing style similar to DOS (such as C:\folder\subfolder), you can change this to display in UNIX format. UNIX format (such as C:/directory/subdirectory/) is commonly found on the Internet and is expected by most Web browsers. Use UNIX format for the greatest compatibility on the Internet.

At A Glance: FTP Listing Styles

Listing Style	Default	Benefit
DOS	Y	easy to use
UNIX	N	compatible with almost everything on Internet

To change your server's directory listing style, perform these steps:

1. From the FTP Site Properties sheet (see the preceding section), click the Home Directory tab (see Figure 2.4).

2. Under Directory Listing Style, select UNIX. The default is MS-DOS.

3. Click OK, or keep this open if you want to continue changing FTP settings.

Now that you have changed your settings, you need to configure your home directory, which is the subject of the next topic.

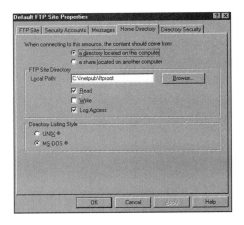

FIGURE 2.4
The Home Directory tab includes settings for changing the directory listing style, as well as other default FTP directory settings.

Configuring FTP Home Directory

IIS 4 enables you to change the home directory for your virtual server. When you install the FTP service, IIS 4 creates a default home directory called \Ftproot. This directory, which has no name and is indicated by a slash (/) in a URL, is the primary location for FTP files.

You place files in the home directory and its subdirectories to enable clients to access them (the files).

To change your home directories, follow these steps:

1. From the FTP Site Properties sheet (see the preceding section), make sure the Home Directory tab appears (refer to Figure 2.4).

2. In the When Connecting to this Resource, the Content Should Come from area, select one of the following paths:

    ◆**A directory located on this computer.** Select this option to specify a local directory.

    ◆**A share located on another computer.** Select this option to specify a directory on another computer on the network.

3. In the Local Path field (or Network Share if you select the second option from the preceding list), enter the path to the directory you want to specify as the home directory. For local directories, use

standard syntax, such as C:\directory\subdirectory. However, network paths must follow the Universal Naming Convention (UNC), such as \\computername\sharename. For shares, enter the username and password to access that computer, if prompted.

4. Set the home directory access controls from the following options:

   ♦**Read.** Lets clients read and download files you store in the home directory or in virtual directories. You must select Read permissions for FTP directories, or every request for a file stored in the home directory will result in an error message being returned to the client. By default, this option is selected.

   ♦**Write.** Lets clients upload files to the home directory on your FTP server. This option should be selected only for FTP servers in which users must upload files. By default, this option is not selected.

   ♦**Log Access.** Provides a record of visitors to the home directory. By default, this option is selected.

5. Click OK.

CONFIGURING IIS TO SUPPORT THE WWW SERVICE

After you install IIS 4.0, you can configure the WWW service for your Web site. Some of the configuration changes you can make include the following:

♦ Setting Bandwidth and User Connections

♦ Setting User Logon Requirements and Authentication Requirements

♦ Modifying Port Settings

♦ Setting Default Pages

♦ Setting HTTP 1.1 Host Header Names to Host Multiple Web Sites

♦ Enabling HTTP Keep-Alives

Setting Bandwidth and User Connections

In order to conserve bandwidth for other clients accessing your Web site, consider limiting the number of connections that can connect to your site. When connection limits are maxed out, those attempting to connect to your server will be rejected and must try again later. You can limit the number of connections to your Web site, FTP site, email, or news servers.

Another task you should consider for your Web site is to limit the bandwidth used by the Web server. This leaves bandwidth available for other services, such as email or news services. Limiting bandwidth is known as *throttling bandwidth*, and limits only the bandwidth used by static HTML files. If you have multiple sites set up, you can throttle the bandwidth used by each site. Bandwidth throttle limits not only HTML files, but all files accessed through the limited Web site. All types of files will be limited to the throughput specified by this setting: GIF, JPG, ASP, HTML, Binaries, and so on.

To set user connections and bandwidth throttling, use these steps:

1. Choose Start, Programs, Windows NT 4.0 Option Pack, Microsoft Internet Information Server, Internet Service Manager.

2. Expand the Internet Information Server folder.

3. Expand the server that you want to modify.

4. Right-click the Default Web Site entry. Your FTP site may be named something different.

5. Click Properties. The Web Site Properties sheet appears.

6. On the Web Site tab, click the Limited To option (see Figure 2.5).

7. Enter a value in the connections field. The default is 1,000, but you may want to lower this if your resources are limited.

8. In the Connection Timeout field, enter a value for the amount of time after which your server should automatically disconnect an idle session. The default is 15 minutes (900 seconds), but an average setting is five minutes (300 seconds). For an infinite amount of time, enter all 9s in this field.

9. Click the Performance tab (see Figure 2.6).

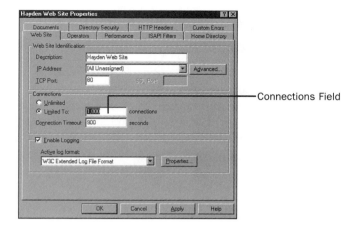

Connections Field

FIGURE 2.5
Use the Web Site tab to set the number of simultaneous connections to your site.

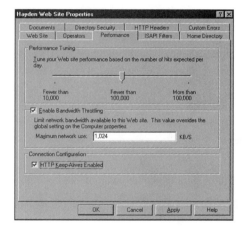

FIGURE 2.6
Set the bandwidth throttling value to limit the bandwidth available to your Web site.

10. Click the Enable Bandwidth Throttling option.

11. In the Maximum network use field, enter a value for the amount of bandwidth (measured in KB/S) you want IIS to use.

12. Click OK, or keep open if you want to continue changing Web site settings.

You have now successfully set the bandwidth throttle for your site.

Setting User Logon Requirements and Authentication Requirements

IIS 4.0 can be set up to verify the identity of clients who access your Web site. On public Web sites on which non-critical or public domain information and applications are available, authentication of users connecting to your Web site may not be important. However, if you have secure data or want to restrict Web access to specific clients, logon and authentication requirements become very important.

Modifying Port Settings

Similar to setting the port for FTP sites, you can change the default port setting for your Web site to any unique TCP port number. If you do this, however, you must let all clients know of your port setting before they can connect to your Web site. For a port setting other than the default, which is 80, the user must enter the port value as part of the URL.

To set the port setting, do these steps:

1. On the Web Site Properties dialog box, click on the Web Site tab (see Figure 2.7).

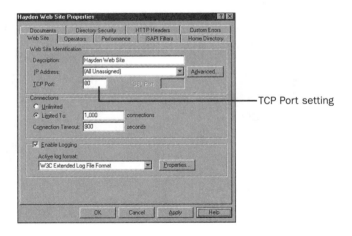

—TCP Port setting

FIGURE 2.7
The default port setting is usually the best for public Web sites, but you can change it by modifying the TCP Port setting on the Web Site tab.

2. In the TCP Port field, enter a new value. This must be a unique TCP value.

3. Click OK, or keep open if you want to continue changing Web site settings.

Setting Default Pages

If you have any experience browsing the Web, you know that for many sites you do not have to enter a specific document name (such as index.html) when accessing many Web sites' home page. You can set IIS 4.0 to display a default page when clients access your site without a specified document in the URL. From this default page (usually your home page or index page), you can direct users to other documents or resources on your site.

IIS 4.0 enables you to specify more then one default document and list them in order of preference. When a client connects to your site, IIS searches for the top-most document and displays it if found. If it can't be found, such as if it is being updated or edited, the next default document is displayed.

To set default pages, use these steps:

1. From the Web Site Properties sheet, click on the Documents tab (see Figure 2.8).

2. Select the Enable Default Document option. This option is enabled by default.

3. Click the Add button to specify a different default document.

4. In the Add Default Document dialog box, specify a new default document. An example of one that many Web sites use is index.htm.

5. Click OK.

6. Click the up or down arrows on the Documents tab to modify the search order for the default documents.

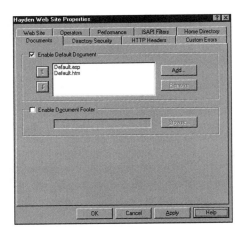

FIGURE 2.8
Setting a default document enables users to connect to your Web site without specifying a document name.

7. Click the Enable Document Footer option if you want IIS to insert an HTML file (which is really a short HTML document with formatting tags for footer content) to the bottom of your Web documents.

8. Enter the path and filename for the footer file.

9. Click OK, or keep open if you want to continue changing Web site settings.

Setting HTTP 1.1 Host Header Names to Host Multiple Web Sites

IIS 4.0 provides support for HTTP 1.1 host headers to allow multiple host names to be associated with one IP address. With this feature, a separate IP address is not needed for every virtual server you support. Microsoft Internet Explorer 3.0 and later and Netscape Navigator 2.0 and later support this feature, but many other browsers do not.

Enabling HTTP Keep-Alives

You can enable IIS 4.0's keep-alive feature to enable clients to maintain open connections. This way a client does not need to re-establish connections for each request. By enabling keep-alive, you decrease the amount of time a client waits to connect to another document or application on your site. But you also increase the amount of resources devoted to this client.

To enable HTTP keep-alives, perform these steps:

1. From the Web Site Properties sheet, click the Performance tab (see Figure 2.9).

2. Select the HTTP Keep-Alives Enabled option. This option is enabled by default. If a check mark already appears in this check box, no changes are needed.

3. Click OK.

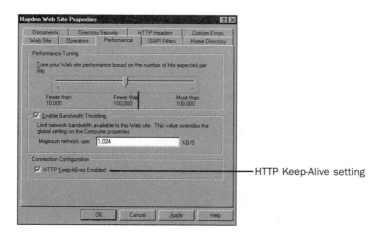

FIGURE 2.9
Enable the HTTP keep-alive setting on the Performance tab.

CONFIGURING AND SAVING CONSOLES BY USING MICROSOFT MANAGEMENT CONSOLE

Microsoft Management Console (MMC) is used to organize and perform management tasks for IIS 4.0. MMC does not actually administer any part of IIS or your network; rather, it provides a framework for other applications (called snap-ins) to administer parts of the network. Internet Service Manager, for instance, is a snap-in. When Internet Service Manager starts (not the HTML version), an MMC console appears with the Internet Service Manager displayed as a snap-in.

In the future, Microsoft BackOffice and Windows NT will offer MMC snap-in administration tools. Other vendors are expected to provide snap-ins as well.

When you start a snap-in in MMC, a console displays. Consoles have one or more windows. The Internet Service Manager, for instance, includes two windows. On the left side, a tree view is shown and is called the scope pane. The right pane, which shows the results of selecting something on the left page, is called the results pane.

You can view multiple windows in the console and then save that view for later. You might, for instance, create one window to show a snap-in for changing settings, while another window displays a Web page with program updates. You can then display that window view or share it with other users via email, floppy disk, or network.

The following steps show how to copy a window view, create a view with a different root, and close the scope pane:

1. Select Start, Programs, Windows NT 4.0 Option Pack, Microsoft Internet Information Server, Internet Service Manager. MMC displays with Internet Service Manager (see Figure 2.10).

2. Select Window, New Window. A copy of the window displays.

3. To create a view with a different root, click the node you want to view as the root.

4. Click the Action menu.

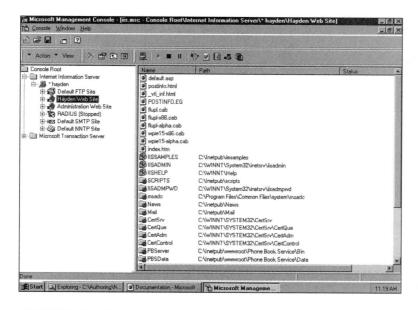

FIGURE 2.10
MMC with Internet Service Manager snap-in displayed.[end fig]

5. Click New Window from here. A new window will appear with the node you select as the root node (see Figure 2.11).

6. To view only the results pane, click the Action menu.

7. Click the Scope Pane option. The scope pane (the left pane) is removed so only the results pane shows.

8. To save this console, select Console, Save As.

9. Fill out the Save As dialog box. Consoles have an MSC extension.

10. Click Save.

You can now view multiple windows in the console and then save that view for later. This allows you to do such things as copy a window view, create a view with a different root, and close the scope pane.

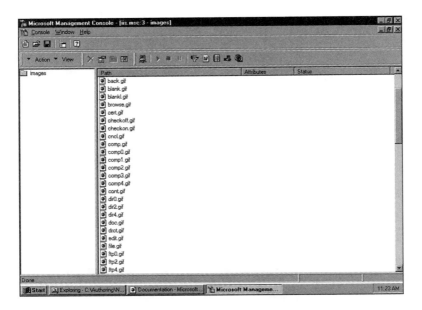

FIGURE 2.11
A node selected as the root node

VERIFYING SERVER SETTINGS BY ACCESSING THE METABASE

The metabase is a memory-resident data storage area that stores your IIS 4.0 configuration values. The metabase is analogous, but not identical, to the Windows NT Registry. It is also faster and more flexible than the Registry. The metabase has keys that correspond to IIS elements; each key has properties that affect the configuration of that element. The hierarchy of the NNTP service keys, for example, looks like the following:

Computer

    NNTP service

        NNTP server

            NNTP virtual directory

You can use the IIS Administration Objects to configure your IIS 4.0 installation, as well as change settings that affect the operation of your IIS Web server, FTP site, virtual directories, and other components. One application that uses the IIS Administration in Objects is the Internet Service Manager (HTML) that you use in Internet Explorer 4 (see Figure 2.12).

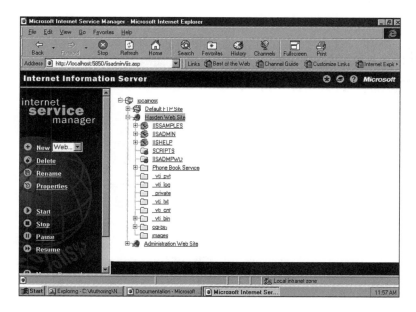

FIGURE 2.12
The HTML version of Internet Service Manager uses IIS Administration Objects to configure IIS components.

CHOOSING THE APPROPRIATE ADMINISTRATION METHOD

IIS 4.0 provides two main ways to administer your IIS installation. You still must use the common Windows NT administration tools to set file and directory rights, user accounts, and view performance measurements. But to administer IIS 4.0, you use Internet Service Manager, either as a snap-in to MMC or as an HTML application in Internet Explorer 4.0.

With Internet Service Manager (HTML), you can manage your Web site remotely using a standard Web browser (IE 4.0 is recommended). This makes it convenient for administrators to manage a Web site when physically away from the site. An administrator, for instance, may be located in a different building than where the Web server is housed. By using Internet Service Manager (HTML), the administrator can connect to the server and administer it from the remote location.

Internet Service Manager (HTML) can be customized using Active Server Pages and the IIS Administration Objects. By customizing Internet Service Manager (HTML), or by creating new HTML-based administration tools, ISP's and administrators can create pages for customers or users to modify settings on the Web.

For administration tasks on the server, administrators can use familiar Windows NT Server administration tools, including the following:

- **User Manager for Domains.** Create a new user for your system to access file, print, and Web services.

- **Event Viewer.** Monitor systems events and log application and security events used by the Web server. Event Viewer also can be used to audit access to secure files.

- **Performance Monitor.** Monitor the performance of IIS 4.0, including FTP, Web services, HTTP, and indexing counters. Use Performance Monitor to get a view of server load.

CUSTOMIZING THE INSTALLATION OF MICROSOFT SITE SERVER EXPRESS ANALYSIS CONTENT ANALYZER

The Site Server Express Analysis Content Analyzer (Content Analyzer for short) enables you to create WebMaps to give you a view of your Web site, helping you manage your Web site. WebMaps are graphical representations of resources on your site. These resources can include HTML documents, audio and video files, Java applets, FTP resources, and applications.

Content Analyzer also enables you to manage your links. You can ensure links are included in the resources and that they all work correctly.

When you install IIS 4, you have the option of installing all or part of the Microsoft Site Server Express 2.0 tool. If you choose the Content Analyzer option (refer to Table 2.3), the Analysis-Content subcomponent should be selected if you want to install the Content Analyzer.

The system requirements and recommendations for installing Content Analyzer are shown in Table 2.4.

TABLE 2.4

CONTENT ANALYZER SYSTEM REQUIREMENTS

Component	Requirement	Recommendation
CPU	Intel 486 66 MHz	120 MHz Pentium
RAM	16MB	32MB
Hard disk space	14MB	N/A
Internet Connection	Modem	Direct
Browser	IE 3.0 or later; Netscape Navigator 3.0 or later	IE 4.0
Authoring Tools	Not Required	Recommended
Multimedia Applications	Not Required	Recommended

After IIS 4.0 is installed, you start Content Analyzer by selecting Start, Programs, Windows NT 4.0 Option Pack, Site Server Express 2.0, Content Analyzer. Click the Open WebMap button to display WebMaps in Content Analyzer. A sample WebMap is included, named SAMPLE.WMP. The Content Analyzer displays as shown in Figure 2.13. This screen shows an example of a WebMap created by Content Analyzer and displayed in tree and Cyberbolic views.

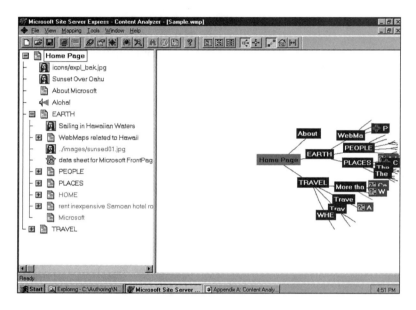

FIGURE 2.13
Most Web site administrators use the tree and Cyberbolic views to view WebMaps.

CUSTOMIZING THE INSTALLATION OF MICROSOFT SITE SERVER ANALYSIS REPORT WRITER AND USAGE IMPORT

Site Server Express includes two types of usage components: the Usage Import (see Figure 2.14) and Report Writer (see Figure 2.15). These tools enable you to gather and review IIS 4.0 log files from a server. With the data you collect from nine different reports, you can chart and identify trends on the usage of your IIS server.

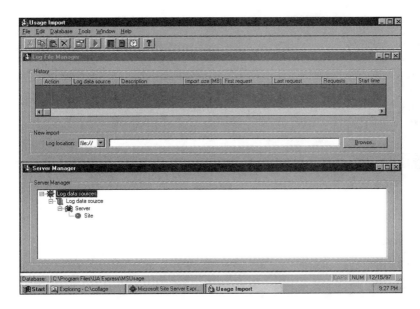

FIGURE 2.14
Usage Import enables you to log data about your IIS 4.0 site.

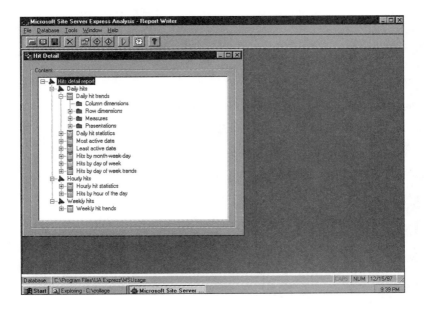

FIGURE 2.15
Report Writer is used to create reports from site data collected by Usage Import and saved in a database.

When you plan to use Usage Import and Report Writer, you should also install a relational database. The database is used to store imported log file data so each of the Site Server Express components can interact with the database to process, organize, and analyze the data. Usage Import is used to filter and configure the data in the database. Report Writer then uses that information to create reports based on the activity on your IIS site.

You can install Report Writer if you choose to install the Site Server Analysis Usage Import component. The system requirements and recommendations for installing Usage Import and Report Writer are shown in Table 2.5.

TABLE 2.5

USAGE IMPORT AND REPORT WRITER SYSTEM REQUIREMENTS

Component	Requirement	Recommendation
CPU	90 MHz Pentium	133 MHz Pentium
RAM	16MB	32MB
Hard disk space	15MB	Additional space for log files needed
Internet Connection	Modem	Direct
Browser	HTML 2-compatible browser that supports tables	IE 4.0

You also may want to install the following optional reporting applications as well:

- Microsoft Word version 7 (or later) to create Word reports

- Microsoft Excel version 7 (or later) to create spreadsheet reports

- Microsoft Access or the Access runtime

- Microsoft SQL Server if the total size of your databases is more than 75MB per month

- Precompiled DLL for Microsoft ISAPI

- Source code for Apache and Netscape NSAPI server extensions

What Is Important to Know

The following bullets summarize the chapter and accentuate the key concepts to memorize for the exam:

- To install IIS 4.0, you must first remove any previous versions of IIS (IIS 3.0, or 2.0 that came with NT 4.0). If Proxy Server has been installed, you must remove it as well. During the installation, you are prompted about which services you want to install.

- If you choose not to install a service at this time, you can restart the installation routine at any time and choose only the additional services you want to add. IIS 4 Hardware Requirements for an Intel System are as follows:

Hardware Device	Requirements
CPU	Minimum of a 50 MHz (90 MHz recommended) 486 DX processor. For bettor performance, you need a Pentium 133 or higher processor.
Hard disk space	Minimum of 50 MB, but it is recommended you have at least 200MB. This does not include storage needed for files you plan to distribute via IIS.
Memory	Minimum of 16MB. For Web sites on which you will store multimedia files or expect a great deal of traffic, 32–64MB is the recommended minimum.
Monitor	Super VGA monitor with 800 × 600 resolution.

- TCP Port settings are used by clients to connect to your FTP or WWW site. Memorize default port settings:

Service	Port
FTP	21
SMTP	25
WWW	80
NNTP	119
SSL	443
NNTP with SSL	563

- You can change the settings to unique TCP port numbers, but you must announce this setting to all clients who want to access your server.

- An FTP directory listing style is the way in which your server will display a directory listing. The two choices are DOS (such as C:\folder\subfolder) or UNIX format (such as C:/directory/subdirectory/). Use UNIX format for the greatest compatibility on the Internet.

- Limiting bandwidth is known as *bandwidth throttling*, and limits only the bandwidth used by the Web service.

- IIS 4.0 provides support for HTTP 1.1 Host Headers in order to allow multiple host names to be associated with one IP address. With this feature, a separate IP address is not needed for every virtual server you support. Microsoft Internet Explorer 3.0 and later and Netscape Navigator 2.0 and later support this feature, but many other browsers do not.

- IIS 4.0's Keep-Alive feature enables clients to maintain open connections. This way, a client does not need to re-establish connections for each request. By enabling Keep-Alives, you decrease the amount of time a client waits to connect to another document or application on your site. But you also increase the amount of resources devoted to this client.

▶ Create and share directories with appropriate permissions. Tasks include:
  - Setting directory-level permissions
  - Setting file-level permission

▶ Create and share local and remote virtual directories with appropriate permissions. Tasks include:
  - Creating a virtual directory and assigning an alias
  - Setting directory-level permissions
  - Setting file-level permissions

▶ Create and share virtual servers with appropriate permissions. Tasks include:
  - Assigning IP addresses

▶ Write scripts to manage the FTP service or the WWW service

▶ Manage a Web site by using Content Analyzer. Tasks include:
  - Creating, customizing, and navigating WebMaps
  - Examining a Web site by using the various reports provided by Content Analyzer
  - Tracking links by using a WebMap

▶ Configure Microsoft SMTP Service to host personal mailboxes

▶ continues...

C H A P T E R 3

Configuring and Managing Resource Access

OBJECTIVES continued

▶ Configure Microsoft NNTP Service to host a news-group

▶ Configure Certificate Server to issue certificates

▶ Configure Index Server to index a Web site

▶ Manage MIME types

▶ Manage the FTP service

▶ Manage the WWW service

CREATING AND SHARING DIRECTORIES

To create and share a new WWW or FTP directory, start the Internet Service Manager and select the server on which you want to create the directory. After that, follow the steps outlined here:

1. Right-click and select New. This brings up the choice of creating an FTP or WWW site. Make the appropriate selection and the corresponding wizard starts. (WWW is used for the rest of this discussion.)

2. Enter the Web site description and select Next.

3. Select or verify the IP address to use.

4. The TCP port defaults to 80. This is the default used for all WWW services. If you want to offer the service but hide it from most browsers, choose another port.

5. If SSL is to be used, enter the appropriate port for it (the default is 443), and click Next.

6. Enter the path for what will appear as the home directory (you can also use the Browse button to specify).

7. By default, the check box appears allowing Anonymous Access to This Web Site (see Figure 3.1). If you do not want anonymous access, remove the check. Choose Next.

8. Select the access permissions for the directory. Choices include:

    ◆ Allow Read Access—assigned by default

    ◆ Allow Script Access—assigned by default

    ◆ Allow Execute Access—which includes Script access

    ◆ Allow Write Access—allows files to be written here

    ◆ Allow Directory Browsing—allows directories to be seen and changed

9. Choose Finish.

FIGURE 3.1
Selecting the home directory path and whether anonymous access is allowed.

Choosing the Access Rights

The five rights that you can select for IIS access work in conjunction with all other rights. Like share rights, the IIS rights are *in addition to* NTFS rights, and of greatest value when you are using anonymous access. Allowing Read access lets users view a file if their NTFS permissions also allow this. Taking away Read, however, prevents the user from viewing the file regardless of what NTFS permissions are set.

At A Glance: Access Rights

Permission	Needed for
Execute	Allows for CGI and ISAPI scripts to execute
Script	Sufficient for IDC, IDQ, and ASP

NOTE

As listed previously, the names of the rights are pretty self-explanatory as to what they offer. The only caveats to note are that Read and Script access are assigned by default, and Execute is a superset of Script access.

Changing Permissions and Access for Directories

After the wizard has been run and the directory is configured for site access, you can change permissions and access for individual directories by selecting the directory in Internet Service Manager, right-clicking, and choosing Properties.

Figure 3.2 shows the properties for a directory. Notice that access permissions have now been set to read and write, or any combination thereof, and permissions are now None, Script, or Execute (which includes Script).

Click the Directory Security tab of the directory's properties and you will see that you have three items you can configure:

+ Anonymous Access and Authentication Control

+ Secure Communications

+ IP Address and Domain Name Restrictions

The latter two are discussed later in this chapter in the section "Directory Security Tab." Selecting Edit on the Enabling Anonymous Access portion opens the screen shown in Figure 3.3. From here, you can choose to allow or disallow anonymous access, and (by choosing Edit) the name of the anonymous access account (which defaults to IUSR_*computername*).

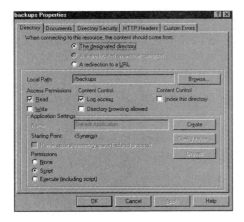

FIGURE 3.2
The properties for a WWW directory.

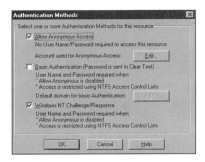

FIGURE 3.3
The Authentication Methods dialog box for the WWW anonymous user.

Changing Permissions and Access for Files

You can also control the permissions for specific files in a similar manner. First, select the file and choose its properties. A screen similar to Figure 3.4 appears. Choosing the File Security tab, you can set the same options for the file as were illustrated in Figure 3.3 for the directory.

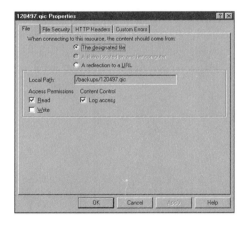

FIGURE 3.4
The properties for a WWW file.

CREATING AND SHARING VIRTUAL DIRECTORIES

As the name implies, virtual directories are entities that do not exist, but give you the ability to reference relative file locations to make it appear as if they are in a directory. In so doing, you can get around issues such as disk space, and determining where best to store files. The biggest disadvantage to using virtual directories, however, is a slight decrease in performance because files must be retrieved from the LAN, rather than being centralized if the virtual directories are on different servers (they need not be). The only other downside is that virtual directories are not visible in directory listings and must be accessed through explicit links within HTML files, or by typing in the complete URL in the browser; for example, `http://www.microsoft.com/iis`.

Virtual directories must exist on servers that all reside within the same NT domain and within the domain in which the IIS server resides. Aside from this restriction, the directories can be either local or remote.

If you choose to create the virtual directory on a local computer, the Internet Service Manager can be used to assign an alias to it. To do so, follow these steps:

1. Start the Internet Service Manager from the Programs portion of the Start menu.

2. Open a Web site, right-click the left pane, and choose New.

3. Select Virtual Directory (as shown in Figure 3.5). This starts the New Virtual Directory Wizard.

4. Enter an alias to be used for the virtual directory name, and click Next (as shown if Figure 3.6).

5. Enter the physical path to the virtual directory as shown in Figure 3.7 (you can also select the Browse button), and click Next.

6. Select the access permissions for the virtual directory. Choices include:

   ◆ Allow Read Access

   ◆ Allow Script Access

♦ Allow Execute Access

♦ Allow Write Access

♦ Allow Directory Browsing

The choices, and defaults, are shown in Figure 3.8.

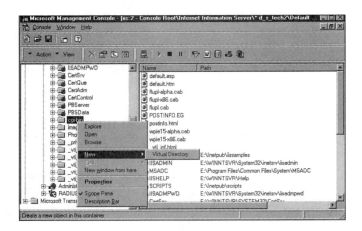

FIGURE 3.5
Select Virtual Directory from the New menu.

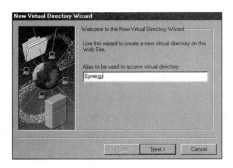

FIGURE 3.6
Enter an alias to be used for the virtual directory.

7. Select Finish.

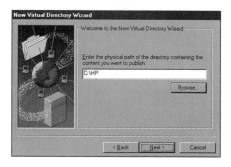

FIGURE 3.7
Enter the physical path for the virtual directory to use.

FIGURE 3.8
Selecting Access rights for the new virtual directory.

After the wizard has been run and the virtual directory is configured for site access, you can change permissions and access for individual directories or files by selecting the directory/file in Internet Service Manager, right-clicking, and choosing Properties.

CREATING AND SHARING VIRTUAL SERVERS

The major benefit of virtual servers is that they allow you to expand your site beyond the limitations of a single site per server. You can combine a number of different sites (domain names) on a single server through the implementation of virtual servers.

Also known as multihomed hosts, multihomed servers, or just plain multihoming, virtual servers allow one host to respond to requests for the following totally different entries:

```
http://www.synergy.com
```

```
http://www.synergy_technology.com
```

and

```
http://www.st.com
```

All the previous domain names are Fully Qualified Domain Names (FQDNs). FQDNs are explained fully in *MCSE Inside Track: TCP/IP* from New Riders Publishing.

Assigning an IP Address

Each site is specified by a unique IP address, and the absence of a unique IP address makes the site visible to all virtual servers.

Creating a Virtual Server

To create a virtual server, you must first have created a directory to publish (local or virtual). Then, follow these steps:

1. Start Internet Service Manager.

2. From the Action menu, select New, and then Web Site (see Figure 3.9).

3. Enter an IP address to use for the site and the TCP port, as shown in Figure 3.10. Click Next.

4. Enter the path for the home directory and whether anonymous access is allowed. Click Next.

5. Configure the appropriate rights, and click Finish.

Permissions for directories and sites on virtual servers can be configured the same as in the previous sections.

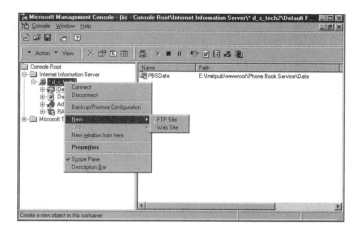

FIGURE 3.9
Creating a virtual server begins with choosing to create a new site.

FIGURE 3.10
Enter the IP address and port for the virtual server.

WRITING SCRIPTS FOR SERVICE MANAGEMENT

New to IIS 4.0 is the Microsoft Script Debugger. It can be used to debug scripts written in JScript, Visual Basic Scripting Edition (VBScript), and a number of other languages. If you know one of these languages, you can simply manage administrative tasks by writing scripts to manage your services (FTP or WWW).

Management tasks to automate should include the inspection of log files (described in "Managing the FTP Service" and "Managing the WWW Service"). The log files can be examined for statistical information such as the number of hits, errors, and so on.

USING CONTENT ANALYZER

The Content Analyzer is a new method of managing your Web site in a simplified manner. It will let you create WebMaps, as shown in Figure 3.11, that let you see a graphical representation of your entire site.

The graphical representation includes all HTML pages, audio and video files, graphic images, and links to other services. The left side of the WebMap display (shown in Figure 3.11) is a tree view of the site, and the right pane shows Cyberbolic view. You can choose to see either of the two, or both, whichever is most convenient for you.

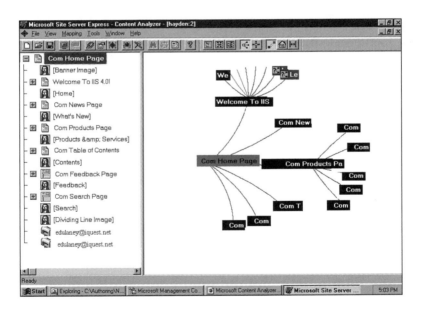

FIGURE 3.11
The WebMap view available in Content Analyzer.

In addition to the graphical representation, Content Analyzer can be used to create a set of links to your site in a report that you can use for troubleshooting. You can also save the maps of your site (to a database, spreadsheet, or HTML file) for comparison at later points in time to see what has changed as time has progressed.

CONFIGURING SMTP

SMTP, an acronym for Simple Mail Transfer Protocol, enables you to send mail to others on your network as well as to the Internet. The SMTP Site property sheet is used to set the basic connection parameters such as the port to use (default port is 25), number of simultaneous connections (default is 1000), and length of inactivity before disconnect (default is 60 seconds).

> **NOTE** A more popular use for the SMTP service is to link its capabilities to a Web page. In other words, if you have a Web site that requires some type of response by the visitor, you can provide a resource for him to use to send you email, without needing a mail client on his end. So, you've given the visitor the power to email you something without requiring him to have an email client such as Outlook installed on their machine.

Regardless of its size, each site has only one Microsoft SMTP site for the service. You cannot create additional sites or delete existing ones. To display the SMTP property sheets, follow these steps:

1. Expand the SMTP tree in Internet Service Manager.

2. Highlight and right-click the SMTP site and choose Properties.

   Five tabs are displayed, as follows:

   ◆ The SMTP Site tab enables you to determine how this server connects to, sends, and receives messages with other servers.

   ◆ The Operators tab enables you to determine which groups have operator status.

- The Messages tab lets you configure limits on message size and decide what to do with undeliverable mail; you can also specify a maximum number of recipients who can receive a single message (the default is 100).

- The Delivery tab specifies how many messages should be sent per connections, the route to use, and so on.

- The Directory Security tab lets you specify other servers to accept only or restrict only.

CONFIGURING NNTP

NNTP, an acronym for Network News Transport Protocol, enables you to configure a server for clients to read newsgroups. The Microsoft NNTP Service included with IIS 4.0 is the server side of the operation, whereas Microsoft Internet Mail and News is a common client (now being replaced in the market by Outlook Express).

The default port for NNTP is 119, although this changes to 563 if SSL is used. When the client connects to the service, it requests a list of available newsgroups. The NNTP service authenticates the user, and then sends the list of newsgroups.

The client picks a newsgroup to view, and requests the list of articles. Authentication takes place again by the NNTP service, and then the list of articles is sent. The client then picks articles she wants to see, and the NNTP Service sends them.

Posting Articles

Posting articles works in a similar fashion: NNTP verifies that the client is allowed to post to the newsgroup, and then takes the article, adds it to the newsgroup, and updates the index.

Every newsgroup has its own directory (with the same name as the newsgroup), and every article is stored as a separate file within that directory (with an .NWS extension). By default, %SystemRoot%\Inetpub\nntproot is the main directory.

Creating a New Newsgroup

When you create a new newsgroup (through the Groups property sheet of Internet Service Manager), NNTP automatically creates the new directory. Within the newsgroup directory, indexes are also stored. They have an extension of .XIX, and one is created for every 128 articles.

The NNTP service starts automatically when the NT Server starts but can be paused, stopped, or started from the Services icon of the Control Panel (where it appears as Microsoft NNTP Service). It, like other IIS-related services, can also be paused, stopped, or started from the Microsoft Management Console.

CONFIGURING CERTIFICATE SERVER

Microsoft Certificate Server enables you to generate, create, and use keys for digital authentication. To use, you must first obtain an industry-recognized server certificate (generated with Key Manager) from a certificate authority. The following is a listing of the Web sites of several certificate authorities within the United States:

Certificate Authorities	Web Site
BankGate	http://www.bankgate.com
GTE CyberTrust	http://www.cybertrust.gte.com
Thawte Consulting	http://www.thawte.com
VeriSign	http://www.verisign.com

> NOTE
>
> You can generate a certificate with Certificate Server without getting certified by an agency, but they aren't considered valid.

After you've created a certificate or a certificate authority has issued you a valid certificate, use Key Manager to activate the certificate.

CONFIGURING INDEX SERVER

Index Server is configured based on the size of the site and the number of documents it contains. Four items should be taken into consideration when configuring Index Server:

- Number of documents in the corpus

- Size of the corpus

- Rate of search requests arriving at the server

- Complexity of queries

Increasing the amount of memory and going with the fastest CPU available will increase Index Server performance. The disk space needed for the data is always roughly 40% the size of the corpus.

Index Server can be used to index multiple servers by sharing a folder on the remote volume and creating a virtual directory on the indexing server. The biggest difficulty in doing this is maintaining link integrity.

MANAGING MIME TYPES

MIME is an acronym for Multipurpose Internet Mail Extension, and is used to define the type of file sent to the browser based on the extension. If your server is supplying files in multiple formats, it must have a MIME mapping for each file type or browsers will most likely be unable to retrieve the file.

MIME mappings for IIS 4.0 are different than they were in previous versions. The mappings are kept in the Registry under KEY_LOCAL_MACHINE\SOFTWARE\Classes\MIME\Databases\ Content Type, and can be viewed, edited, or new ones added by using REGEDIT or REGEDT32. Figure 3.12 shows an example of the MIME mapping for text files in REGEDT32.exe.

These mappings occur whether IIS is installed or not. It appears to be a Windows common registry of MIME types.

If you are not comfortable with editing the Registry directly (and you probably should not be), you can also add entries to the Registry through the HTTP Headers tab of any directory or virtual directory.

FIGURE 3.12
The MIME mapping for text files.

The File Types button at the bottom of the properties page enables you to enter MIME Maps in a much simpler way than editing the Registry. The button is shown in Figure 3.13.

Selecting the Add button enables you to specify new MIME types by giving the associated extension and the content type as shown in Figure 3.14.

FIGURE 3.13
The MIME Map option appears on the HTTP Headers tab.

FIGURE 3.14
The MIME Map option allows you to specify file type extensions and content type.

MANAGING THE FTP SERVICE

Once installed and running, the FTP service can be managed through two main utilities:

- The Services icon of the Control Panel
- Internet Service Manager

Using the Control Panel Method

The first utility of note is the Services icon in the Control Panel. From here, you can start, pause, or stop the FTP Publishing Service, as well as configure it for startup in three ways:

- Automatic (the default)—the service is started when all of IIS starts
- Manual—requires interaction from the administrator to actively start it
- Disabled—it does not start at all

Once started, the service can be stopped or paused (as well as started again after either of the other two). When the service is stopped, it is unloaded, whereas when it is paused, it remains loaded with the intention of it being restarted again.

FTP Site Options with Internet Service Manager

From the Internet Service Manager, you can select your FTP site and choose to stop, pause, or start the site by right-clicking it. You can also manage all properties of the site from here, as shown in Figure 3.15.

There are five tabs to the properties, each containing specific information on the Web site. Each tab is discussed in the paragraphs that follow in the order that they appear by default.

FTP Site Tab

The FTP Site tab enables you to change the description (name) of the FTP site, the IP address, and the TCP port. As has been pointed out before, port 21 is the default TCP port, but changing it to another value allows the site to become "hidden." Additional settings on this tab enable you to specify a number of seconds for a connection timeout, limit the number of connections allowed (if bandwidth is an issue; the default is limited to 1,000 connections), and enable logging. By default, the logs are written to %SystemRoot%\System32\Logfiles.

You can choose for the log files to be created in a number of different time periods. The way in which you choose for them to be created governs the name of the log files created (which always consist of some combination of variables). The following summarizes the log files:

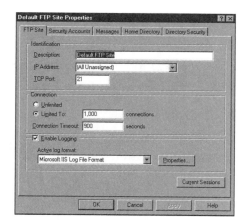

FIGURE 3.15
The Properties sheets for an FTP site.

Log Time Period	Log File Name
Daily	inyymmdd.log
Weekly	inyymmww.log
Monthly	inyymm.log
Unlimited File Size	inetsv#.log
When File Size Reaches... (19MB is the default, but another MB can be specified)	inetsv#.log

Security Accounts Tab

The Security Accounts tab is where you can allow or disallow anonymous access and define which Windows NT user accounts have operator privileges. You can also choose to allow only anonymous connections and enable automatic password synchronization.

At A Glance: Anonymous Only Access

Access	Steps Required	Note
Anonymous only	2	You cannot configure only anonymous access until you have first enabled anonymous access

Messages Tab

The Messages tab allows you to specify a message to be displayed when users access the site. This can be done in three ways:

- Upon welcome
- Upon exit
- Upon there being too many users (maximum connections reached)

Home Directory Tab

The Home Directory tab lets you specify a home directory in either of two ways:

- ◆ On this computer (the default)
- ◆ As a share on another computer

If you are specifying a directory on this computer, you must give the path. If you are specifying a share on another computer, you must give the UNC path (\\server\share). In either scenario, you then assign permissions for that directory of Read and/or Write, and choose whether you want to log access. You also must specify whether directory listings should appear in UNIX style or MS-DOS style. UNIX should be chosen in most implementations for maximum compatibility.

Directory Security Tab

The Directory Security tab allows you to configure IP address and Domain Name restrictions. When configuring, you have two choices:

- ◆ Specify all addresses that are prohibited
- ◆ Specify all addresses that are allowed access

Recall that the three ways to enter addresses are as a single computer (by IP address), a group of computers (by IP address), or by domain name. Refer to Chapter 1, "Planning," for more information about entering addresses.

MANAGING THE WWW SERVICE

Once installed and running, the WWW service can be managed through two main utilities: the Services icon of the Control Panel and the Internet Service Manager. Each of these utilities is discussed in the following sections.

Using the Control Panel Method

The first utility of note is the Services icon in the Control Panel. From here, you can start, pause, or stop the World Wide Web Publishing Service, or configure it for startup in three ways:

- Automatic (the default)—the service is started when all of IIS starts

- Manual—requires interaction from the administrator to actively start it

- Disabled—it does not start at all

Using the Internet Service Manager

From the Internet Service Manager, you can select your Web site (or any Web site if you have multiples) and choose to stop, pause, or start the site by right-clicking it.

You can also manage all properties of the site from here, as shown in Figure 3.16.

There are nine tabs to the properties, each containing specific information of the Web site. In order of how they appear by default, each tab is discussed in the paragraphs that follow.

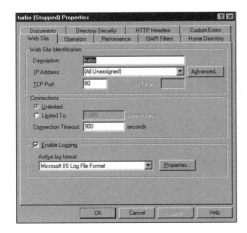

FIGURE 3.16
The Properties sheets for a Web site.

Web Site Tab

The Web Site tab enables you to change the description (name) of the Web site, the IP address, and the TCP port. As has been pointed out before, port 80 is the default TCP port, but changing it to another value allows the site to become "hidden." This is useful in a situation where you want to create an intranet and avoid traffic from the Internet. The Advanced tab will allow you to assign multiple identities for the Web site. Additional settings on this tab enable you to configure the SSL port, limit the number of connections allowed (if bandwidth is an issue; the default is unlimited), and enable logging. By default, the logs are written to:

```
%SystemRoot%\System32\Logfiles
```

You can choose for the log files to be created in a number of different time periods, identical for those already presented for FTP. The way in which you choose for them to be created governs the name of the log files created (which always consist of some combination of variables).

Operators Tab

The Operators tab simply allows you to define which Windows NT user accounts have operator privileges.

Performance Tab

The Performance tab allows you to tune the Web site according to the number of hits you expect each day. There are three settings:

- Fewer than 10,000
- Fewer than 100,000 (the default)
- More than 100,000

You can also enable bandwidth throttling from the Performance tab to prevent the entire network from being slow to service the Web site. By default, bandwidth throttling is not enabled. Finally, on the Performance tab you can configure HTTP keep-alives to be enabled. This maintains the open connection and uses it for the next account, rather than having to create a new connection each time a user accesses the site.

ISAPI Filters Tab

The ISAPI Filters tab enables you to add or remove filters for the site. ISAPI filters are discussed in great detail in Chapter 5, "Running Applications."

Home Directory Tab

The Home Directory tab lets you specify a home directory in three ways:

- On this computer (the default)
- As a share on another computer
- As an URL to be redirected to

If you are specifying a directory on this computer, you must give the path. If you are specifying a share on another computer, you must give the UNC path (*computername**sharename*). In either scenario, you then assign permissions for that directory. If you go with the third option and redirect the home directory to an URL, you must specify the URL and choose how the client will be sent. You can send the client as:

- The exact URL you enter
- A directory below the URL you enter
- A permanent redirection for the resource

Documents Tab

The Documents tab enables you to define the default documents to display if a specific document is not specified in the URL request.

Directory Security Tab

The Directory Security tab enables you to configure Anonymous Access and authentication, as well as Secure Communications and IP address and Domain Name restrictions. When configuring the latter, you have two choices:

- Specify all addresses that are prohibited
- Specify all addresses that are allowed access

The three ways to enter addresses are as a single computer (by IP address), a group of computers (by IP address), or by domain name.

HTTP Headers Tab

The HTTP Headers tab enables you to specify an expiration time for your content (the default is none), set custom headers, assign a rating to your content (to alert parents of pornography, and so on), and configure MIME maps (see the section "Managing MIME Types").

Custom Errors Tab

The last tab, Custom Errors, enables you to configure the error message returned to the user when an event occurs. For example, error 400 is, by default, a Bad Request, and the file 400.htm is used to return the message 404 is Not Found, and so on.

WHAT IS IMPORTANT TO KNOW

The following bullets summarize the chapter and accentuate the key concepts to memorize for the exam:

- The Microsoft Management Console is the primary utility used for most tasks. Accessed by choosing Internet Service Manager from the Programs menu, it is used for almost everything, including creating and sharing new directories or virtual directories, or servers.

- Access permissions for directories include:
  - Allow Read Access
  - Allow Script Access
  - Allow Execute Access
  - Allow Write Access
  - Allow Directory Browsing

- The five rights that you can select for IIS access work in conjunction with all other rights. Like share rights, the IIS rights are *in addition to* NTFS rights, and of greatest value when you are using anonymous access. Allowing Read access lets a user view a file if her NTFS permissions also allowed such. Taking away Read, however, prevents the user from viewing the file regardless of what NTFS may do.

- Read and Script access are assigned by default, and Execute is a superset of Script access.

- With virtual directories, you can get around issues such as disk space, determining where best to store files, and so on.

- There are two downfalls to using virtual directories:

  1. A slight decrease in performance as files must be retrieved from the LAN, rather than being centralized.

  2. Virtual directories do not show up in WWW listings, and must be accessed through explicit links within HTML files, or by typing the complete URL in the browser; for example, `http://www.microsoft.com/ii`

- You should also have a scripts directory under every virtual home directory to handle the executables there.

- The Internet Service Manager (HTML) can let you manage the FTP and WWW service remotely (WWW must first be running in order to use).

- ◆ Remotely, you can do almost everything you can locally with the exception of making MIME Registry changes or stopping and starting services (if you stopped WWW, you would be disconnected).

- ◆ MIME is used to define the type of file sent to the browser based on the extension. If your server is supplying files in multiple formats, it must have a MIME mapping for each file type or browsers will most likely be unable to retrieve the file. Mappings can be added or changed with REGEDIT or REGEDT32.

▶ Configure IIS to connect to a database. Tasks include:
  • Configuring ODBC

▶ Configure IIS to integrate with Index Server. Tasks include:
  • Specifying query parameters by creating the .IDQ file
  • Specifying how the query results are formatted and displayed to the user by creating the .HTX file

CHAPTER 4

Integration and Interoperability

CONFIGURING IIS TO CONNECT TO A DATABASE

With the expansion of the World Wide Web into homes around the United States came the expectation that Web browsers would allow users to retrieve data specific to a need. Users grew frustrated looking at static screen pages and wanted to be able to pull up data and forms based upon a request they had. From an HTML coding standpoint, creating a Web page for every conceivable request is not only impossible, but also impractical. The sheer volume of pages would be incomprehensible, and the action of updating the pages each time a piece of data changed would be more than any one person could handle.

To solve the problem, databases such as Oracle or Microsoft SQL (Structured Query Language) Server can be used with Microsoft Internet Information Server (IIS) 4.0. The databases can supply the information to fulfill a query, update information, and add new data through the Web almost as easily as if a user were sitting at a PC on a local area network.

Databases have been around since the early days of computing, and Web servers have been around for a number of years. What is new is the integration of the two together to create the dynamic Web sites expected today.

Because Windows NT Server is growing in popularity exponentially, and it is the platform on which Internet Information Server runs, it is not uncommon to expect the database to which you connect to be Microsoft SQL Server. This is the expectation for the exam and the thrust of the discussion that follows.

Understanding ODBC

Open Database Connectivity (ODBC) is an API (Application Programming Interface) that provides a simple way to connect to an existing database (whether that database be SQL or any ODBC-compliant database). It was designed by Microsoft to provide a standard for connecting to databases. ODBC can be used to connect to SQL servers, but it was initially designed to provide connectivity to a broad range of databases.

The greatest advantage that ODBC offers is that it defines a clear distinction between the application and the database, and thus does not require any specific programming. To use it, you create a query and template for how the output is to look.

There are four major components to IIS's implementation of ODBC, and they are:

- .HTM—the file containing the hyperlink for a query. The request comes from the browser and merely specifies the URL for the .IDC (Internet Database Connector) file on IIS.

- .IDC—the file containing the data source file information and SQL statement.

- .HTX—a file of HTML extensions containing the template document with placeholders for the result.

- Httpodbc.dll—the dynamic link library included with the server. It handles ODBC requests initiated from IDC files.

Figure 4.1 illustrates the processes involved in answering a query request.

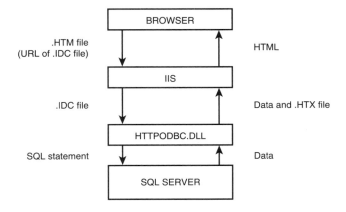

FIGURE 4.1
The process of resolving a database query in IIS.

Implementing ODBC

Implementing ODBC is extremely easy and can be broken into the following steps:

1. Double-click the ODBC icon in the Control Panel.

2. Select the System DSN tab from the ODBC Data Source Administrator dialog box (shown in Figure 4.2).

3. Choose Add and select the driver (SQL, Access, and Oracle appear as choices). This is illustrated in Figure 4.3.

4. Specify the name and description of the data source on the Create a New Data Source dialog box shown in Figure 4.4.

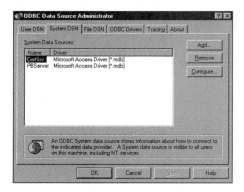

FIGURE 4.2
The System DNS tab enables you to configure data sources.

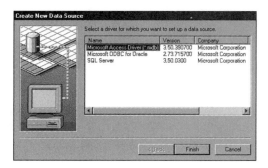

FIGURE 4.3
Select the new data sources.

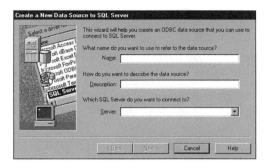

FIGURE 4.4
You must specify a name, description, and server for the data source.

5. Specify the server to connect to and click Next.

6. If you are using a data source that can perform authentication, such as SQL Server, specify how authentication is to be done (see Figure 4.5).

Authentication can be done by Windows NT or SQL Server. If SQL Server is chosen, it uses standard logon security and a SQL Server user ID and password must be given for all connections. If you choose to use Windows NT authentication, the Windows NT user account is associated with a SQL Server user account, and integrated security is used to establish the connection.

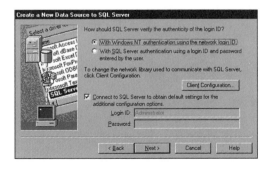

FIGURE 4.5
Specify how authentication will be handled.

NOTE

In reality, to get Windows NT logins to work three things must be done:

- ◆ SQL Server security must be set to Integrated (NT Only) or Mixed (NT & SQL)

- ◆ Named Pipes or Multiprotocol must be set up as the connection type—this is due to the fact that Windows NT refuses to send your password as clear text.

- ◆ You must use SQL Security Manager to assign NT users to SQL users.

The security mode on the server is critical.

Figure 4.5 also shows a Client Configuration button. This can be used to customize the configuration if you are using nonstandard pipes and so on.

The Login ID and Password boxes at the bottom of Figure 4.5 are used only if you have selected SQL Server authentication, and become grayed out if you are using Windows NT authentication.

Other tabs in the ODBC Data Source Administrator dialog box include:

- ◆ User DSN

- ◆ File DSN

- ◆ ODBC Drivers

- ◆ Tracing

- ◆ About

The User DSN tab, shown in Figure 4.6, is used to add, delete, or change the setup of data source names (DSNs). The data sources specified here are local to a computer and can only be used by the current user.

The File DSN tab is used to add, delete, or change the setup of data sources with file data source names. File-based data sources can be shared between all users that are using the same drivers and are not dedicated to individual users or local machines.

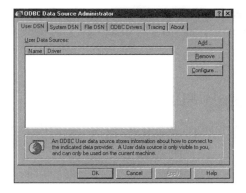

FIGURE 4.6
The User DNS tab enables you to configure data sources specific to a user.

The ODBC Drivers tab shows information about the ODBC drivers that are currently installed. The information given includes the name, version, filename, and created date of every ODBC driver (and the name of the company responsible for it.)

The Tracing tab, shown in Figure 4.7, lets you configure how the ODBC Driver Manager will trace ODBC calls to functions. Choices include all of the time, dynamically, by a custom DLL, or for one connection only (as well as not at all).

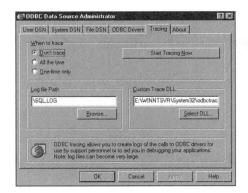

FIGURE 4.7
The Tracing tab of the ODBC Data Source Administrator.

The About tab lists the ODBC core components, as well as the actual file it consists of, and the version. An example of the information it provides is shown in Figure 4.8.

Creating and Developing Files

After the registration has been completed and ODBC configured, the remaining steps involve creating and developing the files to be used.

The .IDC File

The .IDC file contains the SQL command used to interface between IIS and the Httpodbc.dll library. There are four required parameters to the file:

- Datasource
- Username
- Template
- SQLStatement

The Datasource is simply the name of the ODBC data source that has been defined in the ODBC Data Source Administrator dialog box available from the Control Panel.

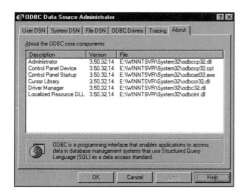

FIGURE 4.8
The About tab of the ODBC Data Source Administrator.

The Username is the user name required to access the datasource, and can be any valid logon name for the SQL Server database. This (as well as the Password field, if used) is ignored if you use integrated security or if the database doesn't have security installed.

The Template specifies the name of the file (.HTX) that will be used as a template to display (and do any necessary interpretation) the SQL results.

The SQLStatement is the list of commands you want to execute. Parameter values can be used if they are enclosed in percents (%), and if multiple lines are required, a plus sign (+) must be the first character on each line.

An example of an .IDC file would be:

```
Datasource: Synergy
Username:   sa
Template:   syn_temp.htx
SQLStatement:
+SELECT employeeno, dob, doh
+FROM pubs.dbo.synergy
+WHERE salary>50000
```

This code will pull the employee number, date of birth, and date of hire information from the pubs.dbo.synergy database for every employee exceeding $50,000 in salary. When the data has been extracted, it is sent combined with an .HTX file (in this case syn_temp.htx) for formatting.

Optional fields that can be used in the .IDC file include:

- DefaultParameters—to specify default values in the event nothing is specified by the client

- Expires—the number of seconds to wait before refreshing

- MaxFieldSize—the maximum buffer space per field (beyond this, truncation takes place)

- MaxRecords—the maximum number of records to return per query

- ODBCConnection—can either be set to POOL or NONPOOL to add the connection to the connection pool (keeping open for future requests) or not do so

- Password—the password for the given user name

- RequiredParameters—parameters that have to be filled in by the client before you can do the query. Parameters are separated by a comma, and if the user does not provide all, Httpodbc.dll returns an error message

- Translationfile—the path for non-English characters to be found before being returned to the browser

- Content-type—a valid MIME type describing what goes back to the client. If the .HTX file has HTML, this is usually "text/html"

The .HTX File

The .HTX file is an HTML template that fills in its blanks with information returned from a query. It accepts SQL information in, and returns HTML information out. A quick look at an .HTX file shows that it looks very much like an HTML file, containing many of the same fields.

Database fields that it receives are known as containers and are identified by field names surrounded by percents (%) and braces (<>). Thus the employeeno field that comes from the SQL database is known as <%employeeno%> here.

All processing is done in loops that start with <%begindetail%> and end with <%enddetail%>. Logic can be included with <%if...%> and <%endif%>, as well as <%else%> statements. You can also use the four standard programming operators:

- EQ—equal to

- GT—greater than

- LT—less than

- CONTAINS

An example of an .HTX file would be:

```
<HTML>
<HEAD>
<TITLE>Welcome to Synergy</TITLE>
</HEAD>
<H2>Employees with Salaries greater than $50,000</H2>
<%begindetail%>
<b>Employee number:</b><%employeeno%> <b>Date of birth and
```

```
hire:</b><%dob%>, <%doh%><P>
<%enddetail%>
</HTML>
```

Some useful samples of .HTX files can be found on your system, and located by using the Windows NT Find utility from the Start menu to look for files ending in that extension. Three useful ones for working with Index Server are located in the %systemroot%\system32\ inetsrv\iisadmin\isadmin directory of your system.

CONFIGURING INTEGRATION WITH INDEX SERVER

Index Server has already been examined several times in this book, including the explanation of it in Chapter 1, and how to configure it in Chapter 3. In this section, we are concerned with how it handles queries and returns results. For most intents and purposes, it is very much like the earlier discussion of .HTX files (used to format and return the query results to the user).

The difference exists in the files used to hold the queries. Rather than using the .IDC file previously discussed, Index Server uses an .IDQ (Internet Data Query) file. The .IDQ file should always be placed in the Scripts directory, and it requires Execute or Script permission to properly function.

There are two sections to the file and it begins with a tag of [Query] (the first section) and followed by the [Names] section. The Names section is purely optional and not used most of the time. If it is used, it defines nonstandard column names that are referred to in a query. The Query section of the file is all that is required, and it can contain parameters, variables, and conditional expressions.

Restrictions are that lines must start with the variable you are trying to set, and only one variable can be set per line. Additionally, percents (%) are used to identify the variables and references.

Variables

The variables that can be used in .IDQ files are as follows:

- CiCatalog—sets the location for the catalog. If the value is already set, the value here overrides that one.

- CiCodepage—sets the server's code page. Again, if the value is already set, the entry here overrides the previous one.

- CiColumns—defines a list of columns that will be used in the .HTX file.

- CiDeferNonIndexedTrimming—by default is not used, but can be set if the scope of the query must be limited.

- CiFlags—query flags can be set to DEEP or SHALLOW to determine if only the directory listed in CiScope is searched or more.

- CiForceUseCi—by setting to TRUE, you can force the query to use the content index even if it is out of date.

- CiLocale—specifies the locale used to issue the query.

- CiMaxRecordsInResultSet—specifies the maximum number of results that can be returned from the query.

- CiMaxRecordsPerPage—specifies the maximum number of records that can appear on a display page.

- CiRestriction—a restriction that you are placing on the query.

- CiScope—specifies the starting directory for the search.

- CiSort—specifies whether the results should be sorted in an ascending or descending order.

- CiTemplate—specifies the full path of the .HTX file from the root. Index Server is bound by the Windows NT shell limit of 260 characters per path.

As with most script files, a pound sign (#) can be used to specify a comment. At whatever point the # sign is in the line, the rest of the line will be ignored.

Conditional Expressions

The conditional expressions that can be used in .IDQ files are the following:

- CONTAINS—is true if any part of the first value is found in the second value

- EQ—equal to

- GE—greater than or equal to

- GT—greater than

- ISEMPTY—is true if the value is null

- LE—less than or equal to

- LT—less than

- NE—not equal to

Example of .IDQ file

An example of an .IDQ file follows:

```
[Query]
CiColumns=employeeno,dob,doh
CiMaxRecordsInResultSet=50
CiMaxRecordsPerPage=20
#20 used for compatibility with most browsers
CiScope=/
CiFlags=DEEP
CiTemplate=/scripts/synergy.htx
```

In the example, three columns are queried in the database: employeeno, dob, and doh. The maximum number of records that will be returned is 50, with up to 20 on each page of display. The fifth line is a comment line added by the person who created the file, to refer to at a later point in time. It has no effect on operation whatsoever. The CiScope is set to the root directory with the search (CiFlags) set to go through all subdirectories. The template to use is then specified by the CiTemplate variable.

WHAT IS IMPORTANT TO KNOW

The following bullets summarize the chapter and accentuate the key concepts to memorize for the exam:

- Databases such as Oracle or Microsoft SQL (Structured Query Language) Server can be used with IIS to supply the information to fulfill a query, update information, and add new data through the Web almost as easily as if a user were sitting on a local area network.

- Open Database Connectivity (ODBC) is an API (Application Programming Interface) that provides a simple way to connect to an existing database (whether that database is SQL or any ODBC-compliant database).

- The greatest advantage that ODBC offers is that it defines a clear distinction between the application and the database, and thus does not require any specific programming. To use it, you create a query and template for how the output is to look.

- There are four major components to IIS's implementation of ODBC:

  - .HTM—the file containing the hyperlink for a query. The request comes from the browser and merely specifies the URL for the .IDC (Internet Database Connector) file on IIS.

  - .HTX—a file of HTML extensions containing the template document with placeholders for the result. Database fields that it receives are known as containers, and are identified by field names surrounded by percents (%) and braces (<>). Thus the `employeeno` field that comes from the SQL database is known as `<%employeeno%>` here. All processing is done in loops that start with `<%begindetail%>` and end with `<%enddetail%>`. Logic can be included with `<%if...%>` and `<%endif%>`, as well as `<%else%>` statements.

  - .IDC—the file containing the data source file information and SQL statement. Four required parameters are `Datasource`, `Username`, `Template`, and `SQLStatement`. The `SQLStatement` is the list of commands you want to execute. Parameter values can be used if they are enclosed in percents (%), and if multiple lines are required, a plus sign (+) must be the first character on each line.

  - Httpodbc.dll—the dynamic link library included with the server.

- Index Server differs from the ODBC discussion in the files used to hold the queries.

- Rather than using the .IDC file, Index Server uses an .IDQ (Internet Data Query) file.

- The .IDQ file should always be placed in the Scripts directory, and it requires Execute or Script permission to properly function.

- There are two sections to the .IDQ file and it begins with a tag of [Query] (the first section) followed by the [Names] section.

- .IDQ restrictions are that lines must start with the variable you are trying to set, and only one variable can be set per line. Additionally, percents (%) are used to identify the variables and references.

- With most script files, a pound sign (#) can be used to specify a comment. At whatever point the # sign is in the line, the rest of the line will be ignored.

OBJECTIVES

▶ Configure IIS to support server-side scripting

▶ Configure IIS to run ISAPI applications

▶ Configure IIS to support ADO associated with the WWW service

CHAPTER 5

Running Applications

CONFIGURING IIS TO SUPPORT SERVER-SIDE SCRIPTING

Microsoft Internet Information Server (IIS) 4.0 allows an administrator or Web master to use Active Server Pages (ASP) to do Web application programming. ASP simplifies server-side programming and offers support for ActiveX objects (also known as server-side objects), as well as HTML tags and all Active scripting commands.

The .ASP extension is assigned to all ASP scripts, and the files include text, HTML tags and ASP script commands. While HTML tags begin with < and end with >, ASP tags begin with <% and end with %>. The tags are also known as *delimiters;* they signal the server that processing is required at that point. For example:

```
It is now <%= Time %>
```

will appear as:

```
It is now 14:52:10
```

The easiest way to create ASP files is to start with standard HTML files and add the script commands to them (as well as rename the file from .HTM to .ASP). For the purposes of passing the exam, also know that *primary script commands* are those within <%%>.

Active Server Pages can be used with VBScript, JScript, PerlScript, or any other recognized scripting language. Not only can you use a variety of languages, but you can also use multiple languages within the same script. The syntax for so doing is:

```
<SCRIPT LANGUAGE="VBScript" RUNAT=SERVER>
routine
</SCRIPT>
<SCRIPT LANGUAGE="PerlScript" RUNAT=SERVER>
routine
</SCRIPT>
```

In addition to defining variables by an operation (such as DATE, TIME, and so on), you can also set variables and reference them within the scripts. This is done with the SET command, and the variable is then referenced in a manner similar to how the TIME variable was referenced. You can also create an array of data to reference with the Session variable, which is unique for the life of the session. For example:

```
Session ("City") = "Anderson"
Set Session ("State") = "IN"
How is the weather in <%= Session("City") %>?
```

will appear as:

```
How is the weather in Anderson?
```

As mentioned above, the Session variables are kept for the entire duration of the session, and abandoned afterward. To force the purging of the variables, you can use the Session.Abandon call. This will lose the variables (as well as end the session).

Understanding Cookies

Clients using ASP first establish unique session keys, a process carried by the use of HTTP cookies. No buffering is used, by default, so all operations that take place are immediately sent to the browser. This causes a session cookie to be sent for every browser interaction, but you can elect to turn on buffering and prevent the sending of some unnecessary cookies.

Walking Through the Steps Involved in Active Server Pages

The following is a simplified example of how ASPs work:

1. The browser sends an HTTP request for an Active Server Page. The server knows it to be an Active Server Page because of the .ASP extension.

2. The server sends the file to ASP.DLL for execution of all code.

3. Processing is done, and the server sends back an HTML page.

4. If there is any client-side code, it is executed on the client, and the page is displayed in the browser. No server-side scripting is sent to the client, so they can't view the script.

Scripting Hosts

There are two scripting hosts available with IIS:

- A Command-based scripting host
- A Windows-based scripting host

The hosts are very similar in nature, with the Command-based one called by Cscript.exe, and the Windows-based host called by Wscript.exe.

Parameters that can be used with Cscript.exe are

- //?—shows the command-line parameters.
- //B—places the engine in batch mode.
- //C—causes Cscript to be the default engine used by running scripts.
- //I—the opposite of //B, it places the engine in interactive mode.
- //logo—shows a logo at execution time.
- //nologo—does not display a logo at execution time.
- //R—registers known script extensions with the engine. Known script extensions include .JS, .VBS, and .TCL. This operation is done by default and you need not use the parameter.
- //S—saves the current command-line options for the user.
- //T:nn—the timeout specified in number of seconds. The default is no limit, but you can specify a value to prevent excessive script execution.

Figure 5.1 shows the Wscript configuration screen (available from the Run command or any command line).

The options for Wscript configuration enable you to specify a number of seconds after which to stop script execution (equivalent to //T:nn in Cscript, and toggling on and off of the banner (//logo and //nologo in Cscript).

FIGURE 5.1
The Wscript configuration box.

Adding Conditions

You can add conditional processing to your scripts by using If..Then..Else logic. The syntax is as follows:

```
If {condition exists} Then
{action to perform}
Else
{another action to perform}
End If
```

You can also run an operation a number of times by using For..Next loops as shown below:

```
For Each {variable} in {set}
{action to perform}
Next
```

As with most scripting languages, indentation is not required, but used to make it easier to read and debug the script. Additionally, ASP itself is not case sensitive, but the language used to execute the commands may be.

Reviewing an Example of Server-Side Scripting

The following is an example based on a script file that Microsoft included with IIS. The Shortcut.vbs file uses Wscript to create a NotePad shortcut on the desktop:

```
' Windows Script Host Sample Script
'
' _____
'               Copyright 1996 Microsoft Corporation
'
' You have a royalty-free right to use, modify, reproduce and
➥distribute
' the Sample Application Files (and/or any modified version) in any
➥way
' you find useful, provided that you agree that Microsoft has no
➥warranty,
' obligations or liability for any Sample Application Files.
' _____
'
' This sample demonstrates how to use the WshShell object.
' to create a shortcut on the desktop


Dim WshShell, MyShortcut, MyDesktop, DesktopPath

' Initialize WshShell object
  Set WshShell = WScript.CreateObject("WScript.Shell")

' Read desktop path using WshSpecialFolders object
  DesktopPath = WshShell.SpecialFolders("Desktop")

' Create a shortcut object on the desktop
  Set MyShortcut = WshShell.CreateShortcut(DesktopPath & "\Shortcut
➥to notepad.lnk")

' Set shortcut object properties and save it
  MyShortcut.TargetPath =
➥WshShell.ExpandEnvironmentStrings("%windir%\notepad.exe")
  MyShortcut.WorkingDirectory =
➥WshShell.ExpandEnvironmentStrings("%windir%")
  MyShortcut.WindowStyle = 4
  MyShortcut.IconLocation =
➥WshShell.ExpandEnvironmentStrings("%windir%\notepad.exe, 0")
  MyShortcut.Save
```

This file is located in the samples directory created during the installation of IIS 4.

Configuring IIS to Run ISAPI Applications

ISAPI—Internet Server API (Application Programming Interface)—applications are an alternative to Active Server Pages. In fact, the ASP scripting engine is an ISAPI filter. Like ASP, ISAPI can be used to write applications that Web users can activate by filling out an HTML form or clicking a link in an HTML page on your Web server. The user-supplied information can then be responded to and the results returned in an HTML page or posted to a database.

ISAPI was a Microsoft improvement over popular CGI (Common Gateway Interface) scripting, and offers much better performance than CGI because applications are loaded into memory at server runtime. This means that they require less overhead and each request does not start a separate process. Additionally, ISAPI applications are created as DLLs on the server, and allow pre-processing of requests and post-processing of responses, permitting site-specific handling of HTTP requests and responses.

ISAPI filters can be used for applications such as customized authentication, access, or logging. You can create complex sites by combining ISAPI filters and applications.

ISAPI works with OLE connectivity and the Internet Database Connector. This allows ISAPI to be implemented as a DLL (in essence, an executable) or as a filter (translating another executable's output). If ISAPI is used as a filter, it is not called by the browser accessing an URL, but rather summoned by the server in response to an event (which could easily be an URL request). Common uses of ISAPI filters include:

- Tracking URL usage statistics
- Performing authentication
- Adding entries to log files
- Compression

NOTE If you want to become an ISAPI programmer, you'll need a book three times the length of this one to learn the language. If you want to pass the exam (the purpose of this book), there are several things you need to know:

- ISAPI applications effectively extend server applications to the desktop

- ISAPI is similar to CGI but offers better performance

- Although created by Microsoft, ISAPI is an open specification that third-parties can write to

- ISAPI filters can do pre- or post-processing

CONFIGURING ADO SUPPORT

The newest enhancement to Microsoft's Web service offering is ADO—ActiveX Data Objects. ADO combines a set of core functions and unique functions for each implementation. ADO was designed to replace the need for all other data access methods, and Microsoft recommends migration of all applications to ADO when it is feasible.

ADO can access:

- Text

- Relational databases

- Any ODBC-compliant data source

ADO grew out of ASP and offers the following benefits:

- Low memory overhead

- Small disk footprint

- Ease of use

- De-emphasis on object hierarchy

- Ability to use ODBC 3.0 connection pooling

The connection pooling referred to enables you to open database connections and manage sharing across different user requests, while reducing the number of idle connections. To use it, you must set a time-out property in the Registry. When a user times out, rather than the connection being totally lost, it is saved into a pool. When the next request comes in, that connection is used, rather than a whole new connection being created each and every time.

Although ADO has a number of benefits, its greatest downside is that it is mostly read-only on the browser. All filtering and processing must be done on the server, and once it reaches the browser, it is in its final state. While there are ways around this, they are more cumbersome and difficult than with other options.

NOTE

As with ISAPI, if you want to become a programmer, you'll need a book three times the length of this one to learn the language. If you want to pass the exam, there are several things you need to know:

- ◆ ADO objects are small, compact, and easy to write

- ◆ ADO knows what data to access through DSN (Data Source Name) files

- ◆ The DSN contains the user security, database configuration, and location information

- ◆ The DSN can be an actual file (text) or merely an entry in the Registry. ODBC allows you to create three types of DSNs—User (in Registry), System (in Registry), or File (text file)

- ◆ A system DSN applies to all users logged into the server

- ◆ A user DSN applies to a specific user (or set of users)

- ◆ A file DSN gives access to multiple users and can be transferred between servers by copying the file

- ◆ DSN files (discussed earlier) are created through the ODBC icon of the Control Panel

- ◆ ADO connections are written in the files as cn. For example:

```
Set cn = Server.CreateObject("ADODB.Connection")
Cn.Open "FILEDSN=Example.dsn"
```

- ◆ A recordset is a subset of the object that you want to retrieve. Rather than retrieving the entire database, you retrieve a component of it, known as a RecordSet object.

- ◆ ADO commands are written in the files as cm. For example:

```
Set cm = Server.CreateObject("ADODB.Command")
Cm.CommandText = "APPEND INTO Array (X, Y) VALUES"
```

WHAT IS IMPORTANT TO KNOW

The following bullets summarize the chapter and accentuate the key concepts to memorize for the exam:

- ISAPI applications effectively extend server applications to the desktop
- ISAPI is similar to CGI but offers better performance; CGI needs a new process for every execution
- Although created by Microsoft, ISAPI is an open specification that third-parties can write to
- ISAPI filters can do pre- or post-processing
- Execute, but not necessarily read permission, is required for CGI or ISAPI script execution

▶ Maintain a log for fine-tuning and auditing purposes. Tasks include:
- Importing log files into a Usage Import and Report Writer Database
- Configuring the logging features of the WWW service
- Configuring the logging features of the FTP service
- Configuring Usage Import and Report Writer to analyze logs created by the WWW service or the FTP service

▶ Monitor performance of various functions by using Performance Monitor. Functions include HHTP and FTP sessions.

▶ Analyze performance. Performance issues include:
- Identifying bottlenecks
- Identifying network-related performance issues
- Identifying disk-related performance issues
- Identifying CPU-related performance issues

▶ Optimize performance of IIS

▶ Optimize performance of Index Server

▶ Optimize performance of Microsoft SMTP Service

▶ Optimize performance of Microsoft NNTP Service

▶ Interpret performance Data

▶ Optimize a Web Site by using Content Analyzer

CHAPTER 6

Monitoring and Optimization

MAINTAINING IIS 4.0 LOGS

Maintaining IIS 4.0 logs is one of the most important tasks in fine-tuning and auditing an IIS site. In the following sections, you learn how to configure WWW and FTP services logging, configure Report Writer and Usage Import to analyze logs created by these services, and automate the Report Writer and Usage Import.

Importing Log Files Into a Report Writer and Usage Import Database

The Report Writer and Usage Import Database help you analyze and create reports based on logs created by IIS. The main difference between Report Writer and Usage Import is that Report Writer creates analysis reports based on the log file data. Usage Import, on the other hand, reads the log files and places the data into a relational database.

To begin using these tools, import the log file or files you want to analyze into a Report Writer and Usage Import database. The database is essentially a container that holds imported data from a log file.

Both Report Writer and Usage Import connect to this database when they start. You can see the name of the database each tool connects to by looking at the bottom of their screens on the status bar (see Figure 6.1). If Report Writer or Usage Import cannot find the database it is configured to connect to, you are prompted to enter the name of a valid database.

Relational databases are used because of their efficient use of data storage. Relational databases do not require redundant information from your log file to be stored. This results in smaller databases and less required disk space. In some cases, the database may be 10–20 percent smaller than the original log file.

Another reason relational databases are used is because they enable you to analyze your data in a more flexible way. You can cross reference over 200 different Internet server usage data properties.

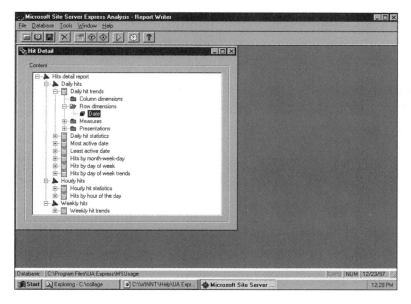

FIGURE 6.1
You can view the database that Report Writer connects to by looking at the status bar.

To import log files into Usage Import, follow these steps:

1. Make sure you can access the Internet server log file on the local computer.

2. Select Start, Programs, Windows NT 4.0 Option Pack, Microsoft Site Server Express 2.0, Usage Import. Usage Import starts. The first time you start Usage Import, you need to configure an Internet site in a database because no sites are configured yet. Usage Import displays the Microsoft Site Server Express Analysis dialog box (see Figure 6.2), which informs you that you must use the Server Manager to configure your Internet site.

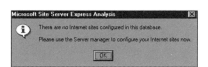

FIGURE 6.2
The Microsoft Site Server Express Analysis dialog box.

3. Click OK. The Log Data Source Properties dialog box displays (see Figure 6.3).

4. From the Log Data Source Properties dialog box, click the log file format for your log data source. Some of the file formats include NCSA Common Log File Format, Microsoft IIS Log File Format, Microsoft IIS Extended Log File Format, W3C Extended Log File Format, and others. The options available here correspond to the type of server you are analyzing. You can read more about the log file types supported in the "Configuring the Logging Features of the WWW Service" and "Configuring the Logging Features of the FTP Service" sections.

5. Click OK. The Server Properties dialog box displays (see Figure 6.4). Set the following items on this dialog box:

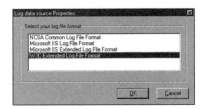

FIGURE 6.3
The Log Data Source Properties dialog box.

FIGURE 6.4
The Server Properties dialog box.

- **Server Type.** Sets the type of server for which your log file is configured. You can select World Wide Web, FTP, Gopher, or RealAudio servers.

- **Directory Index Files.** Enter your server's index file, such as default.asp, index.html, home.htm, or other name. This is the name of the file that is displayed in the client when the URL ends in a /.

- **IP Address.** Enter the IP address of the server. This field is optional.

- **IP Port.** Enter the server's IP port number. The default is 80.

- **Local Timezone.** Enter the local time zone where your content is stored.

- **Local Domain.** Enter the domain name for the local network that is hosting your content. This setting is used to distinguish hits from internal and external clients. If you use a hosting service (such as Iquest), enter the domain of that service, such as iquest.net.

6. Click OK. The Site Properties dialog box displays (see Figure 6.5).

7. Enter the URL of the home page in the Home Page URLs field on the Basics tab. This information is required. As an optional entry, fill in the Server Filesystem Paths for this Site field. If you have multiple URLs, list all of them in this field.

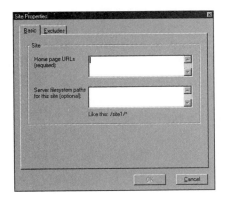

FIGURE 6.5
The Site Properties dialog box.

8. Click the Excludes tab (see Figure 6.6). Here you can set log file information that should be excluded from the database. These settings are optional. You can enter the names of hosts you want to exclude in the Hosts To Exclude From Import field. To exclude log file information based on inline image requests, enter the image file types in the Inline Images To Exclude From Import field. Some common file types you might enter here include .gif, .jpg, .jpeg, and .png. You might opt to include these images to decrease the time it takes to import the log file and make the database smaller.

9. Click OK. The Usage Import window displays with the Log File Manager and Server Manager windows displayed (see Figure 6.7). The Log File Manager organizes, filters, and imports log files for analysis. The Server Manager, on the other hand, sets up the site structure for which the logs are imported. Before any data can be imported into a database, the servers and sites that created the log data must be configured in the Service Manager.

10. In the Log File Manager window, enter the complete path for your log file in the Log Location field. Click Browse to locate the file graphically.

11. Click the Start Import button on the Usage Import window toolbar (this tool is a green right-facing arrow). After Usage Import finishes importing the log file, the Microsoft Site Server Express Analysis dialog box displays telling you the import is completed and how long the import process took (see Figure 6.8).

FIGURE 6.6
The Excludes tab on the Site Properties dialog box.

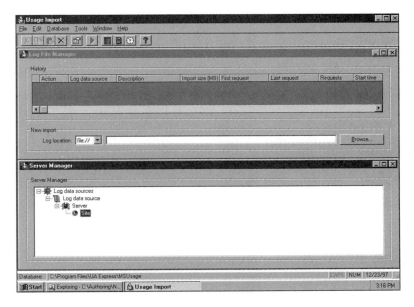

FIGURE 6.7
The Usage Import Window

FIGURE 6.8
The Microsoft Site Server Express Analysis dialog box.

12. Click OK. The Usage Import Statistics dialog box displays (see Figure 6.9).

FIGURE 6.9
The Usage Import Statistics dialog box.

13. Click Close.

When you are ready to create a report of a log file in Report Writer, use these steps:

1. Select Start, Programs, Windows NT 4.0 Option Pack, Microsoft Site Server Express 2.0, Report Writer. Report Writer starts and displays the Report Writer opening dialog box (see Figure 6.10).

2. Select the From the Report Writer Catalog option on the Report Writer dialog box. You can create your own report using the From Scratch option. However, you should use the Report Writer Catalog option the first few times you run Report Writer to see how the tool works.

3. Click OK. The Report Writer dialog box with the Report Writer Catalog field displays (see Figure 6.11).

4. Select the plus sign next to the Detail Reports or Summary Reports folders, depending on the type of summary you want to create.

5. Click a report type, such as Hits detail report. To read about each type of report, click it and view a description in the Report Description area at the bottom of the Report Writer dialog box.

6. Click Next. The Report Writer dialog box shown in Figure 6.12 displays. You set the date range of the data to analyze from this dialog box. The default is Every Request You've Imported. You also can narrow the date ranges, such as This Week, This Year, or a specific range such as Before 12/25/98.

FIGURE 6.10
The Report Writer dialog box.

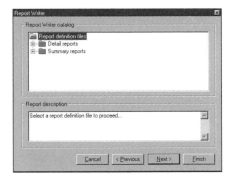

FIGURE 6.11
The Report Writer Catalog field displaying in the Report Writer dialog box.

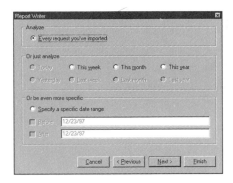

FIGURE 6.12
Set the date range of the log file data to analyze from this Report Writer dialog box.

7. Click Next. The Report Writer dialog box shown in Figure 6.13 displays. From this dialog box, you can filter log file data using Boolean expressions and items included in the Filter Name Reference drop-down list. To use an item in the drop-down list, select the down arrow, click the item, and drag the item to the Filter field. This enables you to create expressions and drag and drop Filter Name Reference items into your expressions.

8. Click Finish. The Detail window for the report you want to generate displays (see Figure 6.14). From this window you can see the types of information that will be included in your new report. You can delete items from this window by selecting the item and pressing Delete.

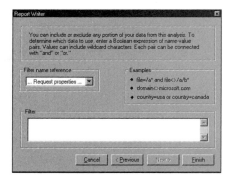

FIGURE 6.13
You can filter log file data using this Report Writer dialog box.

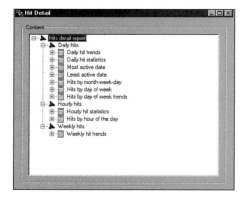

FIGURE 6.14
The Hit Detail window.

9. Click the Create Report Document toolbar button on the Report Writer toolbar. The Report Document dialog box displays (see Figure 6.15).

10. Enter a filename and select the format of the report. The default report format is HTML, which automatically displays in your Web browser. You also can select Microsoft Word and Microsoft Excel, which you can display in those applications. Click the Template button if you want to specify a report template that you have created.

FIGURE 6.15
The Report Document dialog box.

11. Click OK. The report document is created. The Report Writer Statistics dialog box displays as well. Click Close to close this dialog box. If you specified the HTML format in step 10, your registered Web browser will launch with the report displayed (see Figure 6.16).

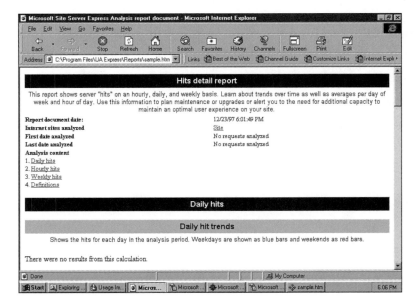

FIGURE 6.16
A Report Writer document displaying in Internet Explorer 4.0.

Configuring the Logging Features of the WWW Service

Probably one of the first actions you want to do when administering your IIS 4.0 site is to configure the logging features of the WWW and FTP services. When looking at log file information, you should keep in mind that this information does not show definitive information about users and visitors to your sites. Internet protocols are stateless, so there cannot be sustained connections between clients and servers.

To configure logging features for your WWW service, use these steps:

1. Select Start, Programs, Windows NT 4.0 Option Pack, Microsoft Internet Information Server, Internet Service Manager. Internet Service Manager opens in the Microsoft Management Console (MMC) (see Figure 6.17).

2. Right-click the Web site you want to configure.

3. Click Properties. The Web Site Properties dialog box displays (see Figure 6.18).

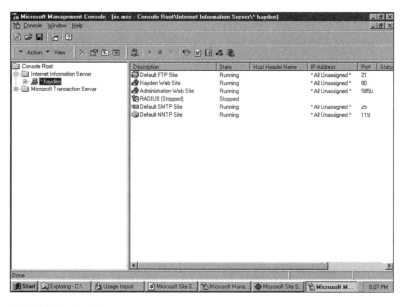

FIGURE 6.17
Internet Service Manager displayed in MMC.

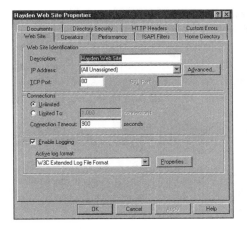

FIGURE 6.18
The Web Site Properties dialog box.

4. Click the Enable Logging option.

5. Click the Active Log Format drop-down list and select the type of log format you want to create. The following are the supported log file formats:

- ◆ **Microsoft IIS Log Format.** This is a fixed ASCII format that records basic logging items, including username, request date, request time, client IP address, number of bytes received, HTTP status code, and other items. This is a comma-delimited log file, making it easier to parse than other ASCII formats.

- ◆ **NCSA Common Log File Format.** This is a fixed ASCII format endorsed by the National Center for Supercomputing Applications (NCSA). The data it logs includes remote hostname, username, HTTP status code, request type, and the number of bytes received by the server. Spaces separate different items logged.

- ◆ **ODBC Logging.** This is a fixed format that is logged to a database. This log includes client IP address, username, request date, request time, HTTP status code, bytes received, bytes sent, action carried out, and the target. When you choose this option, you must specify the database for the file to be logged to. In addition, you must set up the database to receive that log data.

◆ **W3C Extended Log File Format.** This is a customizable ASCII format endorsed by the World Wide Web Consortium (W3C). This is the default setting. You can set this log format to record a number of different settings, such as request date, request time, client IP address, server IP address, server port, HTTP status code, and more. Data is separated by spaces in this format.

The following steps show how to configure the W3C Extended Log File Format.

6. Click the Properties button. The Extended Logging Properties dialog box displays (see Figure 6.19). If you selected a log format other than W3C Extended Log File Format from the Active Log Format drop-down list, the properties dialog box for that format displays.

7. In the New Log Time Period section, set when you want IIS to create a new log file for the selected Web site. The default is Daily, but you can select Weekly, Monthly, Unlimited File Size, or When File Size Reaches. If you select the last option, you need to set a maximum file size the log file can reach before a new file is created. The default here is 19MB. For active Web sites, the log file can reach sizes of over 100MB very quickly.

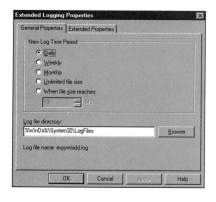

FIGURE 6.19
The Extended Logging Properties dialog box for the W3C Extended Log File Format.

8. Enter the directory in which you want to store the log file. The default is %WinDir\System32\LogFiles. Click the Browse button to locate a new directory graphically.

9. Click the Extended Properties tab to display the logging options (see Figure 6.20) you can set (this tab is available only when you select the W3C Extended Log File Format option). On this tab, you can set the options described in Table 6.1.

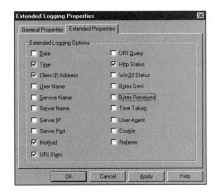

FIGURE 6.20
The Extended Properties tab.

TABLE 6.1

W3C EXTENDED LOG FILE FORMAT LOGGING OPTIONS

Option	Description
Date	Date the activity occurred.
Time	Time activity occurred
Client IP Address	IP address of the client attaching to your server.
User Name	Username who accessed your server.
Service Name	Client computer's Internet service.
Server Name	Server name where the log entry was created.
Server IP	Server IP address where the log entry was created.
Server Port	Shows the port number to which the client is connected.

continues

TABLE 6.1 continued

Option	Description
Method	Shows the action the client was performing.
URI Stem	Logs the resource the client was accessing on your server, such as an HTML page, CGI program, and so on.
URI Query	Logs the search string the client was trying to match.
HTTP Status	Shows the status (in HTTP terms) of the client action.
Win32 Status	Shows the status (in Windows NT terms) of the client action.
Bytes Sent	Shows the number of bytes sent by the server.
Bytes Received	Shows the number of bytes received by the server.
Time Taken	Shows the amount of time to execute the action requested by the client.
User Agent	Reports the browser used by the client.
Cookie	Shows the content of any cookies sent or received by the server.
Protocol Version	Shows the protocol used by the client to access the server (HTTP or FTP)
Referrer	Shows the URL of the site from where the user clicked on to get to your site.

The default Extended Logging Options for the W3C Extended Log File Format include Time, Client IP Address, Method, URI Stem, and HTTP Status.

10. Click OK to close the Extended Logging Properties dialog box.

11. Click OK to close the Web Site Properties dialog box.

Log files can grow very large, so be sure the server on which the log file resides has plenty of free disk space. Logging shuts down if your server runs out of disk space when trying to add a new log entry to a file. When this happens, you'll see an event logged in the Windows NT Event Viewer. Another event will be logged when IIS is able to continue logging IIS activities.

Configuring the Logging Features of the FTP Service

Like the WWW service, you can configure the logging features of the FTP service in IIS 4.0. To do this, use these steps:

1. Select Start, Programs, Windows NT 4.0 Option Pack, Microsoft Internet Information Server, Internet Service Manager. Internet Service Manager opens in the Microsoft Management Console (MMC) (refer to Figure 6.17).

2. Right-click the FTP site you want to configure.

3. Click Properties. The Default FTP Site Properties dialog box displays (see Figure 6.21).

4. Click the Enable Logging option.

5. Click the Active Log Format drop-down list and select the type of log format you want to create. You can choose from Microsoft IIS Log File Format, ODBC Logging, and W3C Extended Log File Formation. NCSA Common Log File Format is not supported on FTP sites. See step 5 in the preceding section for an explanation of these formats.

   The following steps show how to configure the W3C Extended Log File Format.

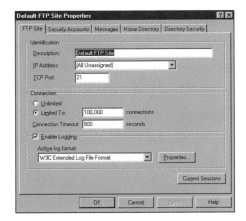

FIGURE 6.21
The Default FTP Site Properties dialog box.

6. Click the Properties button. The Extended Logging Properties dialog box displays (see Figure 6.22). If you selected a log format other than W3C Extended Log File Format from the Active Log Format drop-down list, the properties dialog box for that format displays.

7. In the New Log Time Period section, set when you want IIS to create a new log file for the selected FTP site. The default is Daily, but you can select Weekly, Monthly, Unlimited File Size, or When File Size Reaches. If you select the last option, you need to set a maximum file size the log file can reach before a new file is created. The default here is 19MB.

8. Enter the directory in which you want to store the log file. The default is %WinDir\System32\LogFiles. Click the Browse button to locate a new directory graphically.

9. Click the Extended Properties tab to display the logging options (see Figure 6.23) you can set (this tab is available only when you select the W3C Extended Log File Format option). On this tab, you can set the options described earlier in Table 6.1.

10. Click OK to close the Extended Logging Properties dialog box.

11. Click OK to close the FTP Site Properties dialog box.

FIGURE 6.22
The Extended Logging Properties dialog box for the W3C Extended Log File Format.

FIGURE 6.23
The Extended Properties tab.

Configuring Report Writer and Usage Import to Analyze Logs Created by the WWW Service or the FTP Service

You learned earlier how to import a log file into Usage Import and how to create a report in Report Writer. You learn here how to configure Report Writer and Usage Import to analyze logs that are created by your WWW or FTP service.

The Usage Import Options

In Usage Import, you can access the Usage Import Options dialog box by selecting Tools, Options. This dialog box (see Figure 6.24) enables you to configure several settings and save them as your default settings, or use them only during the current Usage Import session. If you opt not to save them as default settings, the next time you start Usage Import the previous settings are used.

On the Import tab, you can set the following options:

- **Drop Database Indexes.** For analysis purposes, database indexes must be created. After you have a large amount of data in a database, however, you can enable this option and drop indexes during the import process.

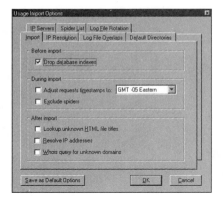

FIGURE 6.24
The Usage Import Options dialog box.

- **Adjust Requests Timestamps To.** Turn on this option if you want all time stamps in log files to adjust to the time zone shown in the drop-down list. This is handy if you have Web sites on servers in multiple time zones.

- **Exclude Spiders.** By selecting this option, you tell IIS to disregard hits from Internet search engines (which use spiders to search the Internet) and other agents shown on the Spider List tab.

- **Lookup Unknown HTML File Titles.** Performs HTML title lookups on HTML files added to the database during the log file import.

- **Resolve IP Addresses.** Resolves unresolved IP addresses found in log files during the import process.

- **Whois Query for Unknown Domains.** Tells Usage Import to perform a Whois query for unknown organization names.

The IP Resolution tab (see Figure 6.25) includes the following options:

- **Cache IP Resolutions for n Days.** Enables you to set the number of days in between IP lookups.

- **Timeout a Resolution Attempt After n Seconds.** Enables you to set the number of seconds for Usage Import to attempt to resolve an IP address. After this time, Usage Import will stop attempting to resolve the IP address. Higher values mean better results, but will slow down the import process.

- ◆ **Use a Resolution Batch Size of n IPs.** Specifies the batch size Usage Import uses for IP resolution.

The Log File Overlaps tab (see Figure 6.26) includes the following two options:

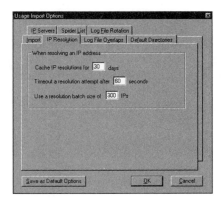

FIGURE 6.25
The IP Resolution tab.

FIGURE 6.26
The Log File Overlaps tab.

◆ **To Be Considered an Overlap, Records Must Overlap By At Least n Minutes.** Sets the overlap period by the import module. Overlap periods are redundancies introduced in your log file database because of log files being accidentally re-imported, resuming interrupted logging actions, concatenating two log files, and running logs on separate servers. If you specify shorter periods, overlaps may be reduced but later analysis may be adversely affected.

◆ **If An Overlap is Detected.** Enables you to choose the action that Usage Import should take when an overlap is detected. You can choose from these options: Import All Records, Stop the Import, Stop All Imports, and Discard Records and Proceed.

The Default Directories tab (see Figure 6.27) includes one option, the Log Files field. Use this field to specify the default directory for log files and import files.

The IP Servers tab (see Figure 6.28) includes these two options:

◆ **HTTP Proxy.** Import uses the proxy server host name (if specified) and Port number for all HTML title lookups.

◆ **Local Domain of DNS Server.** Clarifies hosts returned from IP resolutions. Enter your DNS server here, or, if an ISP maintains your DNS server, enter your ISP's setting here.

FIGURE 6.27
The Default Directories tab.

FIGURE 6.28
The IP Servers tab.

The Spider List tab (see Figure 6.29) includes common spider agents you want to exclude if the Exclude Spiders option is selected on the Import tab. You can delete any agent here by selecting it and pressing Delete. Or, you can add to the list by placing an asterisks (*) after the Freeloader item and then entering the word *and*, followed by the name of the agent. No spaces are allowed between words.

FIGURE 6.29
The Spider List tab.

Finally, the Log File Rotation tab (see Figure 6.30) includes the **At the End of an Import** item. This option enables you to control the treatment of data that is cut off due to file rotation. This is data that is divided at the end of one file and begins again at the start of a new log. You can select from these options: Commit Open Visits To Database, Discard Open Visits, and Store Open Visits for Next Import.

Click OK on the Usage Import Options dialog box to close it and to use the settings you've configured.

Configuring the Report Writer Options

You can configure Report Writer options by opening Report Writer and selecting Tools, Options. The Report Writer Options dialog box displays (see Figure 6.31).

On the Report Contents tab, you can set the following options:

- **Include Within Report.** Use this option to have Report Writer include usage definitions at the bottom of every report. You may, after you become more familiar with Report Writer documents, want to disable this option so your reports don't have these definitions.

- **For Print Clarity, Shade Graphs With.** Use this option to specify Solid Colors and Pattern Lines for graph shading. For printed reports on non–color printers, select the Pattern Lines option.

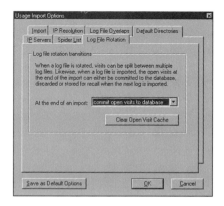

FIGURE 6.30
The Log File Rotation tab.

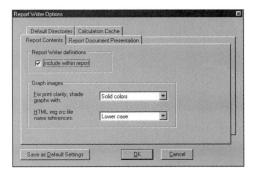

FIGURE 6.31
The Report Writer Options dialog box.

- ◆ **HTML Img Src File Name References.** Select which case to use when naming image and source files. For UNIX systems, use the correct case option for your system. In most situations, Lower Case is the best choice.

On the Report Document Presentation tab (see Figure 6.32), you can set the following options on how the report is styled:

- ◆ **Visible.** Specify this option so Report Writer displays header information, including analysis time period, site analyzed, and report sections.

- ◆ **Font, Color, and Size options.** Use these options to specify the font, color, and size of the header information text.

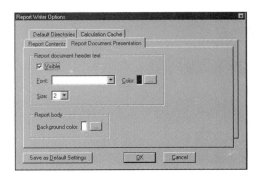

FIGURE 6.32
The Report Document Presentation tab.

◆ **Background Color.** Click the ... button to display the Color dialog box in which to specify a background color for your report.

The Default Directories tab (see Figure 6.33) includes these two options:

◆ **Report Documents.** Set the path for your completed reports in this field.

◆ **Analysis Files.** Set the path for your completed analysis files in this field.

Finally, the Calculation Cache tab (see Figure 6.34) includes these options:

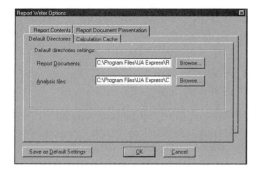

FIGURE 6.33
The Default Directories tab.

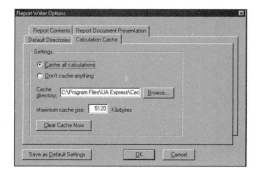

FIGURE 6.34
The Calculations Cache tab.

- **Cache All Calculations.** Enables you to cache report calculations in the Cache folder for future use. By using cache calculations, you can speed up report generations.

- **Don't Cache Anything.** Turns off the calculation cache feature.

- **Cache Directory.** Sets the directory in which calculations are cached.

- **Maximum Cache Size.** Sets the maximum amount of cached material the Cache directory can hold. This setting is in kilobytes.

- **Clear Cache Now.** Click this button when you want to clear the calculations cache.

Click OK to close the Report Writer Options dialog box and use the settings you've configured.

Automating the Use of Report Writer and Usage Import

A handy feature of the Report Writer and Usage Import is the automation capability. Automating Report Writer and Usage Import is done by using the Scheduler tool. You can set up Scheduler so that a report is generated every day when you arrive at work, or a report is created at the end of the week to be dispersed to your Internet site administration team.

When you use Scheduler, you create jobs that have tasks scheduled to begin at specific time and days. Tasks are simply activities, such as importing a log or creating a report. After you set up a job, Scheduler creates a batch file that will run to execute the specific tasks.

To create a new job in Usage Import, follow these steps:

1. Open Usage Import and click on the Scheduler toolbar button (or select Tools, Scheduler). The Scheduler window displays (see Figure 6.35).

2. Double-click the All Jobs item. The Job Properties dialog box displays (see Figure 6.36).

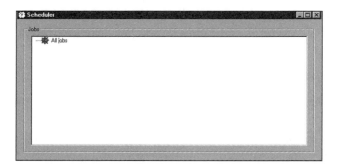

FIGURE 6.35
The Scheduler window.

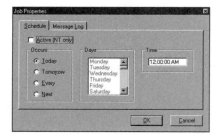

FIGURE 6.36
The Job Properties dialog box.

3. Click the Active (NT Only) check box. If this is cleared, the Scheduler does not run the specified job. This is handy if you want to disable a specific job without deleting it entirely. This way you have the option of enabling it again without going through the process of setting up the job again.

4. In the Occurs area, select when you want the job to start.

5. If you chose Every or Next in the preceding step, select the day(s) you want the job to run in the Days area. Press Ctrl to select multiple days.

6. Enter the time you want the job to run in the Time field.

7. Click the Message Log tab (see Figure 6.37). You can save messages about the results of each task in a log file by entering the path and filename for the log file in the Message Log field. From the

drop-down list, you can select variables to be added to the file-name. When the file is created, the variables, such as $d(23)$, are replaced by actual values.

8. Click OK to save your new job to the Scheduler window (see Figure 6.38).

You now need to add tasks to your new job. Follow these steps:

1. Right-click your new job and select New Task. The Task Properties dialog box displays (see Figure 6.39).

2. Select the type of task you want to add to your job by clicking on the Task Type drop-down list. If you want to automate the data-base compacting tasks, for instance, select Compact database. The options available on the Task Properties dialog box change when you pick a different task.

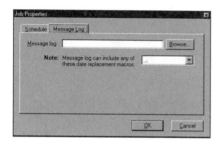

FIGURE 6.37
The Message Log tab.

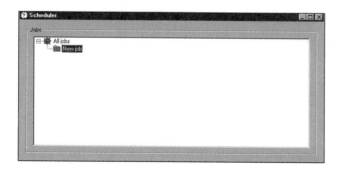

FIGURE 6.38
Your new job added to the Scheduler window.

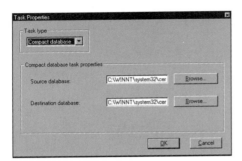

FIGURE 6.39
The Task Properties dialog box.

3. Fill out the fields (if any are shown) for the task you select.

4. Click OK to save your new task. The Scheduler window shows the new task under your new job (see Figure 6.40). Again, you can rename the new task by clicking it twice.

5. Continue adding tasks to your job by repeating steps 1–4.

6. When finished, close the Scheduler window and click Yes when prompted to start the job.

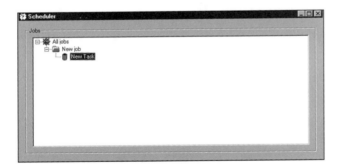

FIGURE 6.40
A New Task added to your new job.

MONITORING PERFORMANCE OF VARIOUS FUNCTIONS USING PERFORMANCE MONITOR

IIS 4.0 provides several powerful tools to monitor and administer your Internet server. But you can still use common Windows NT administration tools to monitor IIS 4.0's performance. One such tool that is indispensable for IIS 4.0 monitoring is Performance Monitor.

With Performance Monitor you can monitor functions relating to HTTP and FTP sessions. Performance Monitor is used when you want to see trends and patterns in your site's usage. When you install IIS 4.0, new objects relating to Web and FTP services are added to Performance Monitor along with specific counters for those services. Objects are individual occurrences of a system resource, such as Web Service, FTP Service, Active Server Pages, Browser, and other items. Counters, on the other hand, are statistics relating to the objects, such as Debugging Requests, Memory Allocated, and Request Wait Time (all of which relate to the Active Server Pages object).

Performance Monitor can be started from the Administrative Tools (Common) folder. To specify the object and counter(s) you want to track, select Edit, Add to Chart. The Add to Chart dialog box displays (see Figure 6.41).

The Performance Monitor screen shown in Figure 6.42 is monitoring functions relating to Web and FTP service. Namely, the following objects and counters are used:

- Web Services object with Anonymous User/sec, Bytes Sent/sec and Maximum NonAnonymous Users counters selected

- FTP Server object with Bytes Total/sec, Current Anonymous Users, and Maximum Connections counters selected

Table 6.2 lists the objects and counters available in Performance Monitor to help you monitor IIS 4.0.

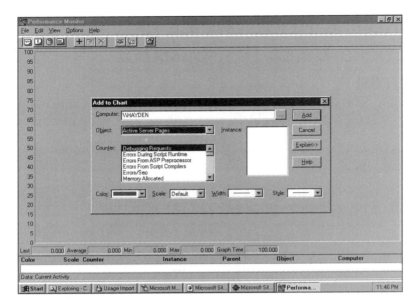

FIGURE 6.41
Add objects and counters to Performance Monitor from the Add to Chart dialog box.

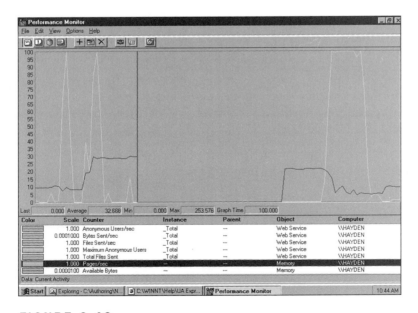

FIGURE 6.42
An example of monitoring Web and FTP services in Performance Monitor.

TABLE 6.2

**IIS 4.0–RELATED OBJECTS AND COUNTERS IN PERFORMANCE
MONITOR**

Object	*Counter*
Active Server Pages	Debugging Requests
	Errors During Script Runtime
	Errors From ASP Preprocessor
	Errors From Script Compilers
	Errors/Sec
	Memory Allocated
	Request Bytes In Total
	Request Bytes Out Total
	Request Execution Time
	Request Wait Time
	Requests Disconnected
	Requests Executing
	Requests Failed Total
	Requests Not Authorized
	Requests Not Found
	Requests Queued
	Requests Rejected
	Requests Succeeded
	Requests Timed Out
	Requests Total
	Requests/Sec
	Script Engines Cached
	Session Duration
	Sessions Current
	Sessions Timed Out
	Sessions Total
	Template Cache Hit Rate

continues

TABLE 6.2 continued

Object	*Counter*
	Template Notifications
	Templates Cached
	Transactions Aborted
	Transactions Committed
	Transactions Pending
	Transactions Total
	Transactions/Sec
FTP Service	Bytes Received/sec
	Bytes Sent/sec
	Bytes Total/sec
	Current Anonymous Users
	Current Connections
	Current NonAnonymous Users
	Maximum Anonymous Users
	Total Anonymous Users
	Total Connection Attempts
	Total Files Received
	Total Files Sent
	Total Files Transferred
	Total Logon Attempts
	Total NonAnonymous Users
Internet Information Services	Cache Flushes Global
	Cache Hits
	Cache Hits %
	Cache Misses
	Cached File Handles
	Current Blocked Async I/O Requests
	Directory Listings

Object	*Counter*
	Measured Async I/O Bandwidth Usage
	Objects
	Total Allowed Async I/O Requests
	Total Blocked Async I/O Requests
	Total Rejected Async I/O Requests
NNTP Server	Article Map Entries
	Article Map Entries/Sec
	Articles Deleted
	Articles Deleted/Sec
	Articles Posted
	Articles Posted/Sec
	Articles Received
	Articles Received/Sec
	Articles Sent
	Articles Sent/Sec
	Articles Total
	Bytes Received/sec
	Bytes Sent/sec
	Bytes Total/sec
	Control Messages Failed
	Control Messages Received
	Current Anonymous Users
	Current Connections
	Current NonAnonymous Users
	Current Outbound Connections
	Failed Outbound Logons
	History Map Entries
	History Map Entries/Sec

continues

TABLE 6.2   continued

Object	*Counter*
	Maximum Anonymous Users
	Maximum Connections
	Maximum NonAnonymous Users
	Moderated Postings Failed
	Moderated Postings Sent
	Sessions Flow Controlled
	Total Anonymous Users
	Total Connections
	Total NonAnonymous Users
	Total Outbound Connections
	Total Outbound Connections Failed
	Total Passive Feeds
	Total Pull Feeds
	Total Push Feeds
	Total SSL Connections
	Xover Entries
	Xover Entries/Sec
SMTP Server	% Recipients Local
	% Recipients Remote
	Avg Recipients/msg Received
	Avg Recipients/msg Sent
	Avg Retries/msg Delivered
	Avg Retries/msg Sent
	Bytes Received Total
	Bytes Received/sec
	Bytes Sent Total
	Bytes Sent/sec
	Bytes Total

Object	*Counter*
	Bytes Total/sec
	Connection Errors/sec
	Directory Drops Total
	Directory Drops/sec
	Directory Pickup Queue Length
	DNS Queries Total
	DNS Queries/sec
	ETRN Messages Total
	ETRN Messages/sec
	Inbound Connections Current
	Inbound Connections Total
	Local Queue Length
	Local Retry Queue Length
	Message Bytes Received Total
	Message Bytes Received/sec
	Message Bytes Sent Total
	Message Bytes Sent/sec
	Message Bytes Total
	Message Bytes Total/sec
	Message Delivery Retries
	Message Received/sec
	Message Send Retries
	Messages Delivered Total
	Messages Delivered/sec
	Messages Received Total
	Messages Refused for Address Objects
	Messages Refused for Mail Objects
	Messages Refused For Size
	Messages Retrieved Total

continues

TABLE 6.2 continued

Object	Counter
	Messages Retrieved/sec
	Messages Sent Total
	Messages Sent/sec
	NDR's Generated
	Number of MailFiles Open
	Number of QueueFiles Open
	Outbound Connections Current
	Outbound Connections Refused
	Outbound Connections Total
	Remote Queue Length
	Remote Retry Queue Length
	Routing Table Lookups Total
	Routing Table Lookups/sec
	Total Connection Errors
Web Service	Anonymous Users/sec
	Bytes Received/sec
	Bytes Sent/sec
	Bytes Total/sec
	CGI Requests/sec
	Connection Attempts/sec
	Current Anonymous Users
	Current Blocked Asyn I/O Requests
	Current CGI Requests
	Current Connections
	Current ISAPI Extension Requests
	Current NonAnonymous Users
	Delete Requests/sec
	Files Received/sec

Object	*Counter*
	Files Sent/sec
	Files/sec
	Get Requests/sec
	Head Requests/sec
	ISAPI Extension Requests/sec
	Logon Attempts/sec
	Maximum Anonymous Users
	Maximum CGI Requests
	Maximum Connections
	Maximum ISAPI Extension Requests
	Maximum NonAnonymous Users
	Measured Async I/O Bandwidth Usage
	NonAnonymous Users/sec
	Not Found Errors/sec
	Other Request Methods/sec
	Post Requests/sec
	Put Requests/sec
	System Code Resident Bytes
	Total Allowed Async I/O Requests
	Total Anonymous Users
	Total Blocked Async I/O Requests
	Total CGI Requests
	Total Connection Attempts
	Total Delete Requests
	Total Files Received
	Total Files Sent
	Total Files Transferred
	Total Get Requests
	Total Head Requests

continues

TABLE 6.2 continued

Object	*Counter*
	Total ISAPI Extension Requests
	Total Logon Attempts
	Total Method Requests
	Total Method Requests/sec
	Total NonAnonymous Users
	Total Not Found Errors
	Total Other Request Methods
	Total Post Requests
	Total Put Requests
	Total Rejected Async I/O Requests
	Total Trace Requests

ANALYZING PERFORMANCE

As the IIS 4.0 administrator, you'll be responsible for analyzing the performance of the Internet site. But you'll also need to pay close attention to other server performance issues. These performance issues include the following:

- Identifying bottlenecks
- Identify network-related performance issues
- Identify disk-related performance issues
- Identify CPU-related performance issues

Identifying Bottlenecks

Bottlenecks occur when one (or several) hardware resource is being used too much, usually resulting in the draining of another hardware resource. The result is a performance reduction over the entire network. A bottleneck may occur as a result of insufficient server memory or because of too little bandwidth available to the connected users. You'll need to know how to recognize bottlenecks on your system before you can even attempt to remedy them.

At A Glance: Bottlenecks

Main Bottleneck Problem	Reason	Solution
Logging to a database	As IIS 4.0 logs activities to a database, an ODBC connection must be established. This connection process may take a relatively long time.	Switch to file-based logging.

Finding a bottleneck can be a slow and arduous task at times. You must don your "detective" hat when looking for the combination of hardware and software that is creating the bottleneck. Start looking for bottlenecks by running Performance Monitor to create a baseline of activities for your site.

You also can use Event Viewer to record events and audit situations on your computer that may require your attention. Another useful tool to use to locate bottlenecks is the Task Manager. Task Manager shows you all the ongoing tasks and threads on your computer.

The following are some common bottlenecks that you should become familiar with when administering IIS 4.0.

Identifying Network-Related Performance Issues

Because IIS 4.0 may reside on your local area network server, you should become aware of some of the network-related performance issues that can affect the performance of your Internet site.

For medium to very busy sites, you can expect IIS to saturate a 10MB Ethernet network adapter. This will certainly cause bottlenecks to occur that are network-related. To check for network saturation, check for CPU % Utilization by looking at the CPU % Processor Time value on both the client and server. To prevent the server from becoming network bound, try one of the following solutions:

- ♦ Use multiple 10MB Ethernet cards, or

- ♦ Install a 100MB Ethernet or FDDI network card.

- ♦ Take advantage of a higher speed BUS architecture, such as upgrading from an ISA card to PCI.

Identifying Disk-Related Performance Issues

You may encounter hard disk bottlenecks if you have a very large file set that is being accessed by clients in a random pattern. To identify a bottleneck of this sort, perform the following steps:

1. Start Performance Monitor.

2. Select Edit, Add To Chart.

3. From the Add To Chart dialog box (see Figure 6.43), select the PhysicalDisk item from the Object drop-down list object.

4. From the Counter list, select % Disk Time.

5. Click Add.

6. Click Done.

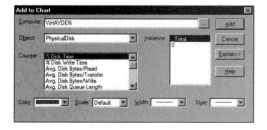

FIGURE 6.43
Select the PhysicalDisk object and % Disk Time counter from the Add To Chart dialog box.

The % Disk Time counter shows the percentage of elapsed time the disk is busy servicing read or write requests. If there is a bottleneck involving disk access, the PhysicalDisk % Disk Time counter will be high. This is a because the percentage of the CPU utilization will remain low and the network card will not be saturated.

When you notice a disk-related bottleneck, you can improve performance by using a redundant array of inexpensive drives (RAID) and striped disk sets.

> **N O T E**
>
> If your disk access is a bottleneck due to database accessing via a Web site, it would be beneficial to relocate the SQL server to another machine. As an added precaution, you could enable NetBEUI or NWLink communication between the two machines to increase security.

Identifying CPU-Related Performance Issues

You can identify CPU bottlenecks by measuring the amount of the server CPU that is being utilized. Use the following steps to measure this value:

1. Start Performance Monitor

2. Select Edit, Add To Chart.

3. From the Add To Chart dialog box, select the Processor item from the Object drop-down list object.

4. From the Counter list, select % Processor Time.

5. From the Instance list, select IIssrv.

6. Click Add.

7. Click Done.

You'll notice CPU bottlenecks if you notice very high CPU % Processor Time numbers while the network card remains well below capacity. If the CPU % Processor Time value is high, try the following remedies:

- Upgrade the CPU to a faster one

- Add additional CPUs to your server

- Move any CPU-intensive applications (such as database applications, or SQL databases) you run on the Web server to another computer.

- Add more computers on which you replicate your site and then distribute traffic across them.

OPTIMIZING THE PERFORMANCE OF IIS

One of the greatest improvements to IIS 4.0 is the inclusion of the Microsoft Management Console (MMC) to help you manage and administer IIS. With MMC, you can make global performance changes (such as limiting bandwidth usage), set service master properties, and configure other IIS properties to help optimize its performance.

To change global performance properties under IIS, use these steps:

1. Open Internet Service Manager in MMC.

2. Right-click the computer you want to modify.

3. Select Properties to display the Server Properties dialog box for that server (see Figure 6.44).

FIGURE 6.44
The Server Properties dialog box.

4. Click the Performance tab, and then the Enable Bandwidth Throttling option, to control the amount of bandwidth consumption by all IIS services. You may want to do this if your network card is set up to handle multiple services, such as email and Web services. In the Maximum Network Use field, enter a bandwidth value in KB/sec (kilobytes/second).

5. Click the Master Properties drop-down list. This displays the services (WWW and/or FTP) you have installed and those for which you can customize default master properties. Master properties are standard settings for all the Web sites or FTP sites hosted on your server. After you set master properties for all your sites, you can still modify settings for individual sites. Master properties provide you with an easy and quick way to set common parameters for all your sites.

6. Select the service you want to modify.

7. Click Edit. The WWW Service Master Properties dialog box for your site displays (see Figure 6.45).

From this dialog box you can set the following performance parameters:

- Connections

- Performance

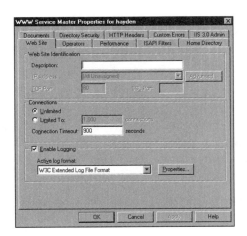

FIGURE 6.45
The WWW Service Master Properties dialog box.

- Enable Bandwidth Throttling
- HTTP Keep-Alives

These parameters are discussed in more detail in the following sections.

Connections

On the Web Site tab of the Service Master Properties dialog box there is a Connections area. This area includes the Unlimited and Limited To options that control the number of simultaneous connections your Web or FTP sites allow. Click the Limited To option to specify the number of simultaneous connections to your sites. Then enter a value in the connection field (the default is 1,000). If you do not want to limit the number of connections, select the Unlimited option (which is the default setting).

You also can set the timeout value for each inactive connection. This value is set in seconds and will automatically disconnect a client after that client has been inactive on your site for the set number of seconds. In the Connection Timeout field, enter a value for the amount of time your server should automatically disconnect an idle session. The default is 15 minutes (900 seconds), but an average setting is five minutes (300 seconds). For an infinite amount of time, enter all 9s in this field.

Performance

The Performance tab (see Figure 6.46) on the Service Master Properties dialog box includes the Performance Tuning option. This option is set to the estimated number of connections you anticipate for your site. Move the Tune slider to the appropriate value. If you anticipate fewer than 10,000 visitors each day, move the slider to the far left; for a site with fewer than 100,000 visitors, keep the slider in the middle; and for a busy site that has over 100,000 visitors, move the slider to the far right.

When you move the slider to a setting, IIS 4.0 alters the resources allocated to the service. Settings that are higher than the actual number of connections will result in faster connections and will improve server performance. This is because more resources are allocated to fewer connections. On the other hand, if you set the Performance Tuning slider to a number that is much higher than the actual number of connections, you will notice a decrease in server performance because server memory is being wasted (basically it is not being utilized). You should compare your daily hit logs with the Performance Tuning setting to ensure this setting closely matches the actual connections to your site.

FIGURE 6.46
The Performance tab on the WWW Service Master Properties dialog box.

Enable Bandwidth Throttling

Another performance option you can set is also on the Performance tab. The Enable Bandwidth Throttling option, which you were shown how to set at the server level in the "Optimizing the Performance of IIS" section, sets the global bandwidth used by your Web site.

Click the Enable Bandwidth Throttling option and set a bandwidth setting based on kilobytes per second (KB/sec).

HTTP Keep-Alives

The final performance optimization setting you can modify on the Performance tab is the Connection Configuration option. This includes the HTTP Keep-Alives Enable option. You can enable IIS 4.0's keep-alive feature to enable clients to maintain open connections. This way a client does not need to re-establish connections for each request, such as for each request for an image, document, or other resource. By enabling keep-alive, you decrease the amount of time a client waits to connect to another document or application on your site. But you also increase the amount of resources devoted to this client.

Click on the HTTP Keep-Alives Enabled option to turn on this feature. By turning on this feature, clients with slower connections are not prematurely closed. You should enable this feature for better server performance so that repeated requests from an individual client are not necessary when a page containing multiple elements is accessed.

Inheritance Overrides

If you make any changes to the WWW Service Master Properties options, you also affect all individual sites under that service. When you click OK to save settings on the Service Master Properties dialog box (see Figure 6.47), the Inheritance Overrides dialog box will appear if a value you've changed will be overridden based on values of an individual site, or *child node*.

Select the child node(s) from the Descendants With Overridden Defaults For the Current Property you want to change to match the new value you set on the Service Master Properties dialog box. Click OK.

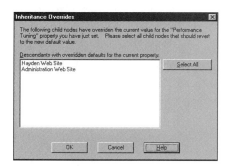

FIGURE 6.47
The Inheritance Overrides dialog box.

Optimizing the Performance of Index Server

At A Glance: Index Server

Minimum Free Disk Space	Recommended Free Disk Space	Index Server Stop
The minimum amount of disk space should be at least 30 percent of the size of your corpus.	During a master merge, you need up to 45 percent of the corpus size.	3MB

Microsoft Index Server is used to index the contents and properties of Internet or intranet documents stored on an IIS server. You are shown how to install Index Server in earlier chapters, but one way to optimize its performance is to run it on a system with an optimum configuration. By and large, the basic Windows NT Server configuration provides adequate Index Server performance. This situation is probably best suited, however, for a small organization or an Internet site that does not expect a large amount of daily traffic.

To optimize the performance of Index Server, you should start by looking at the configuration of the computer on which it resides. The following are the factors that you need to measure to set this configuration:

- Number of documents in the corpus, which is the collection of documents and HTML pages indexed by Index Server

- Corpus size

- Rate of search requests

- Kind of queries

You'll find that the amount of memory you have installed will greatly affect the performance of Index Server. For sites that have fewer than 100,000 documents stored in the corpus, a minimum of 32MB is required and recommended. However, if you have 100,000 to 250,000 documents, the recommended amount of memory jumps to

64–128MB, whereas the minimum required still is 32MB. For sites with 250,000 to 500,000 documents, you need a minimum of 64MB of RAM, but it is recommended that you have 128–256MB. Finally, if you have over 500,000 documents, you must have 128MB of RAM installed, but at least 256MB is recommended.

Another system configuration setting you should pay attention to is the amount of free hard disk space where the Index Server catalog is stored. If less than 3MB of free space is available on the index disk, indexing and filtering are temporarily paused until additional disk space is made available. The event log records a message that `Very low disk space was detected on drive <drive>. Please free up at least <number>MB of space for content index to continue.`

OPTIMIZING THE PERFORMANCE OF MICROSOFT SMTP SERVICE

The Microsoft SMTP service enables IIS 4.0 to deliver messages over the Internet. Microsoft SMTP supports basic SMTP (Simple Mail Transfer Protocol) delivery functions and is compatible with SMTP mail clients.

When you install IIS 4.0, you can also install Microsoft SMTP. The default settings for Microsoft SMTP can be used, but you also can customize your SMTP Service to optimize it for your system. The following are some of the ways you can optimize Microsoft SMTP:

- Set connection limits
- Set message limits
- Specify a smart host

Setting Connection Limits

You can set the number of simultaneous connections for incoming and outgoing connections. To set this number, open Microsoft Manager Console (MMC), right-click the SMTP site you want to modify, and select Properties. The SMTP Site Properties dialog box displays (see Figure 6.48).

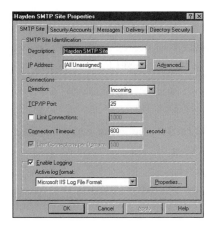

FIGURE 6.48
The SMTP Site Properties dialog box.

On the SMTP Site tab, perform the following steps to set the connection limit:

1. Click the Limit Connections option.

2. In the Limit Connections option field, enter the number of simultaneous connections for your SMTP Service. For incoming messages, the default is 1,000 and the minimum is 1. For outgoing messages, the default is 500 or 1000 and the minimum is 1. Outgoing messages refers to the number of concurrent outbound connections to all remote domains.

3. In the Connection Timeout field, enter the period of time before an inactive connection is disconnected. The default is 600 seconds for both incoming and outgoing messages.

4. In the Limit Connections Per Domain field, enter the number of outgoing connections to a single remote domain. This option is available only with outgoing connections. The default is 100 connections and should be less than or equal to the value set in the Limit Connection field.

5. Click Apply.

Message Limits

You can set limits on the size and number of messages each connection can have. To do this, click the Messages tab of the SMTP Site Properties dialog box (see Figure 6.49) and follow these steps:

1. Click the Limit Messages option.

2. In the Maximum Message Size field, enter the value for the maximum size of a message (in kilobytes). The minimum size is 1KB; the default is 2048KB (2MBs).

3. In the Maximum Session Size field, enter the value for the maximum size of a message before the connection will be closed. Set this value to the same or higher than the Maximum Message Size. The default is 10MB.

4. Click the Limit Messages Per Connections option to specify the number of messages that can be sent in one connection. You can use this value to increase system performance by enabling SMTP Server to use multiple connections to deliver messages to a remote domain. When the limit is reached, a new connection is opened and the transmission continues until all messages are delivered.

5. Click Apply.

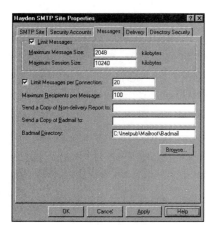

FIGURE 6.49
The Messages tab of the SMTP Site Properties dialog box.

Specifying a Smart Host

Instead of sending all outgoing messages directly to a remote domain, you can route all messages through a smart host. A smart host enables you to route messages over a more direct or less costly connection than via other routes.

To set up a smart host, do the following:

1. Select the Delivery tab (see Figure 6.50) on the SMTP Site Properties dialog box.

2. In the Smart Host field, enter the name of the smart host server. You can enter a string or enter an IP address in this field. To increase system performance when using an IP address here, enclose the address in brackets. Microsoft SMTP will then look at the IP address as an actual IP address without looking at it as a string value first.

3. Select the Attempt Direct Delivery Before Sending to Smart Host option. This option is used if you want SMTP Service to attempt to deliver remote messages locally before forwarding them to the smart host server. The default is to send all remote messages to the smart host, not to attempt direct delivery.

4. Click OK.

FIGURE 6.50
The Delivery tab on the SMTP Site Properties dialog box.

OPTIMIZING THE PERFORMANCE OF MICROSOFT NNTP SERVICE

The Microsoft NNTP Service is used to let users exchange communications via the Internet Network News Transport Protocol (NNTP). Users can post and view articles, much like they can when attached to the Usenet news service available on the Internet.

Similar to the Microsoft SMTP Server, you can run Microsoft NNTP Service without modifying its default settings. However, you may want to tweak some of its properties to get better performance out of it. Two optimization tasks you can perform include changing connection settings and modifying client postings.

Changing Connection Settings

You can limit the number of simultaneous news client connections to a virtual server. You can set a value up to 2 billion, in other words, a relatively unlimited number of connections. To do this, open the Microsoft Management Console and right-click the NNTP Site you want to modify. Select Properties to display the NNTP Site Properties dialog box (see Figure 6.51).

On the News Site tab, follow these steps:

1. Click the Unlimited option, if you want to specify that there is no limit to the number of simultaneous connections.

2. Click the Limited To option and fill in the connections field with the number of simultaneous connections you want to limit NNTP to handling. The default is 5,000. Increase or decrease this value depending on your server size and needs.

3. In the Connection Timeout field, enter a value for NNTP Server to automatically disconnect inactive clients. The default is 600 seconds.

4. Click Apply.

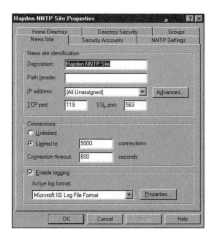

FIGURE 6.51
The NNTP Site Properties dialog box.

Modifying Client Postings

The NNTP Settings tab (see Figure 6.52) includes options for modifying client posting parameters. This tab lets you set the maximum size of news articles posted to your NNTP Server.

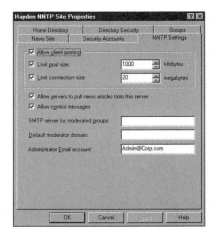

FIGURE 6.52
The NNTP Settings tab.

To modify client postings, use these steps:

1. Select the Limit Post Size option.

2. Enter a value to indicate the maximum size of a news article that a client can post to your NNTP Server. The default is 1,000KB. However, you may want to decrease this value if you want your news server to be set up to handle smaller articles. Increase this value, on the other hand, to allow larger articles to be posted. If an article exceeds this value, it still will be posted if the article does not surpass the Limit Connection Size value.

3. Click the Limit Connection Size option.

4. Enter a value to indicate the maximum size for articles that a news client can post to your news server. The default is 20MB.

5. Click OK.

OPTIMIZING A WEB SITE USING CONTENT ANALYZER

The Site Server Express Analysis Content Analyzer (Content Analyzer for short) enables you to create WebMaps to give you a view of your Web site, helping you manage your Web site. WebMaps are graphical representations of resources on your site. These resources can include HTML documents, audio and video files, Java applets, FTP resources, and applications. Content Analyzer also enables you to manage your links. You can ensure links are included in the resources and that they all work correctly.

You can use Content Analyzer to optimize your Web site. Some of the ways you can do this follow:

* Import usage data to review how users are using your site (see Figure 6.53). Important data you can view here includes how many hits a page receives, which pages are being hit the most, and from which URLs those hits coming.

* Export the Tree view of your site's WebMap to be an HTML index or table of contents for your site. You also can use the index report from the Content Analyzer site report to serve as an HTML index of your site's contents.

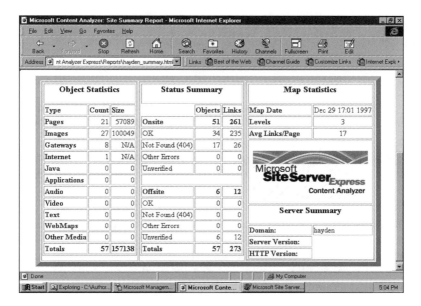

FIGURE 6.53
Content Analyzer provides a report of your site.

- Assign helper applications to file types to edit source files. From Content Analyzer you can set helper applications to create and view site resources. This helps you quickly check a broken link and fix it in an HTML editor such as Microsoft FrontPage.

- View resource properties from within Content Analyzer. You can view the name, size, load size, modification date, URL, MIME type, HTTP status, and other properties.

- View a resource's links in Content Analyzer. When viewing links within a resource, you can see the hyperlink text, MIME type, size, order, HTTP status, number of links, location of the linked document, hits, and other link information. Use this information to fine-tune or fix link-related problems in your documents.

- Verify onsite and offsite links using Content Analyzer. Links that are unavailable are shown in red. These links may be broken, or an offsite link may not have been available when you attempted to verify it.

WHAT IS IMPORTANT TO KNOW

The following bullets summarize the chapter and accentuate the key concepts to memorize for the exam:

- The Active Log Format drop-down list lets you select the type of log format you want to create. The following are the supported log file formats:

  - Microsoft IIS Log Format. This is a fixed ASCII format that records basic logging items, including username, request date, request time, client IP address, number of bytes received, HTTP status code, and other items. This is a comma-delimited log file, making it easier to parse than other ASCII formats.

  - NCSA Common Log File Format. This is a fixed ASCII format endorsed by the National Center for Supercomputing Applications (NCSA). The data it logs includes remote hostname, username, HTTP status code, request type, and the number of bytes received by the server. Spaces separate different items logged.

  - ODBC Logging. This is a fixed format that is logged to a database. This log includes client IP address, username, request date, request time, HTTP status code, bytes received, bytes sent, action carried out, and the target. When you choose this option, you must specify the database for the file to be logged to. In addition, you must set up the database to receive that log data.

  - W3C Extended Log File Format. This is a customizable ASCII format endorsed by the World Wide Web Consortium (W3C). This is the default setting. You can set this log format to record a number of different settings, such as request date, request time, client IP address, server IP address, server port, HTTP status code, and more. Data is separated by spaces in this format.

- In the New Log Time Period section of the site's configuration, you set when you want IIS to create a new log file for the selected Web site. The default is Daily, but you can select Weekly, Monthly, Unlimited File Size, or When File Size Reaches. If you select the last option, you need to set a maximum file size that the log file can reach before a new file is created. The default is 19MB. The default directory in which you store log files is %WinDir\System32\LogFiles.

- The Report Writer and Usage Import Database help you analyze and create reports based on logs created by IIS. The main difference between Report Writer and Usage Import is that Report Writer creates analysis reports based on the log file data. Usage Import, on the other hand, reads the log files and places the data into a relational database.

◆ Performance Monitor is used when you want to see trends and patterns of your site's usage. When you install IIS, new objects relating to Web and FTP services are added to Performance Monitor along with specific counters for those services. Objects are individual occurrences of a system resource, such as Web Service, FTP Service, Active Server Pages, Browser, and other items. Counters, on the other hand, are statistics relating to the objects, such as Debugging Requests, Memory Allocated, and Request Wait Time (all of which relate to the Active Server Pages object).

◆ Bottlenecks occur when one (or several) hardware resource is being used too much, usually resulting in the draining of another hardware resource. The result is a performance reduction over the entire network. A bottleneck may occur as a result of insufficient server memory or because of too little bandwidth available to the connected users.

◆ Start looking for bottlenecks by running Performance Monitor to create a baseline of activities for your site. You also can use Event Viewer to record events and audit situations on your computer that may require your attention. Another useful tool to use to locate bottlenecks is the Task Manager. Task Manager shows you all the ongoing tasks and threads on your computer.

◆ For medium to very busy sites, you can expect IIS to saturate a 10MB Ethernet network adapter. This will certainly cause bottlenecks to occur that are network-related. To check for network saturation, check for CPU % Utilization on both the client and server. To prevent the server from becoming network bound, try one of the following solutions:

  • Use multiple 10MB Ethernet cards, or

  • Install a 100MB Ethernet or FDDI network card.

◆ CPU bottlenecks can be identified by measuring the amount of the server CPU that is being utilized. If the CPU % Processor Time value is high, try the following remedies:

  • Upgrade the CPU to a faster one

  • Add additional CPUs to your server

  • Move any CPU-intensive applications (such as database applications) you run on the Web server to another computer.

  • Add more computers on which you replicate your site and then distribute traffic across them.

◆ To optimize the performance of Index Server, you should start by looking at the configuration of the computer on which it resides. The following are the factors that you need to measure to set this configuration:

- Number of documents in the corpus, which is the collection of documents and HTML pages indexed by Index Server.

- Corpus size

- Rate of search requests

- Kind of queries

♦ You'll find that the amount of memory you have installed will greatly affect the performance of Index Server. For sites that have fewer than 100,000 documents stored in the corpus, a minimum of 32MB is required and recommended. However, if you have over 100,000 up to 250,000 documents, the recommended amount of memory jumps to 64–128MB, whereas the minimum required still is 32MB. For sites with 250,000 to 500,000 documents, you need a minimum of 64MB of RAM, but it is recommended that you have 128–256MB. Finally, if you have over 500,000 documents, you must have 128MB of RAM installed, but at least 256MB is recommended.

▶ Resolve IIS configuration problems

▶ Resolve security problems

▶ Resolve resource access problems

▶ Resolve Index Server query problems

▶ Resolve setup issues when installing IIS on a Windows NT 4.0 computer

▶ Use a WebMap to find and repair broken links, hyperlink texts, headings, and titles

▶ Resolve WWW service problems

▶ Resolve FTP service problems

CHAPTER 7

Troubleshooting

RESOLVING IIS CONFIGURATION PROBLEMS

IIS configuration problems can usually be diagnosed rather quickly by the fact that nothing works. If the problem is not with configuration (such as security, Index Server, and so on), the problem is isolated to those services. If the problem is configuration, however, everything ceases to operate.

Configuration problems can be related to the installation of IIS or the configuration of TCP/IP. We will look at each of these in the following sections.

Installation Problems

Before you set up IIS 4, your system must meet or exceed the hardware requirements summarized in Tables 7.1 and 7.2. Table 7.1 shows requirements for a system running an Intel x86 processor; Table 7.2 lists requirements for a system running a DEC Alpha processor.

TABLE 7.1

IIS 4 HARDWARE REQUIREMENTS FOR AN INTEL SYSTEM

Hardware Device	Requirements
CPU	Minimum of a 50MHZ 486 DX processor (90MHZ recommended). For better performance, you need a Pentium 133 or higher processor.
Hard disk space	Minimum of 50MB, but it is recommended you have at least 200MB. This does not include storage needed for files you plan to distribute via IIS.
Memory	Minimum of 16MB (32 to 64MB recommended). For a Web site on which you will store multimedia files or expect a great deal of traffic, 48MB is the recommended minimum.
Monitor	Super VGA monitor with 800×600 resolution.

TABLE 7.2

IIS 4 HARDWARE REQUIREMENTS FOR AN ALPHA SYSTEM

Hardware Device	Requirements
CPU	Minimum of 150MHZ processor (200MHZ recommended).
Hard disk space	Minimum of 50MB , but you should allocate up to 200MB for best performance.
Memory	Minimum of 48MB. For better performance, have at least 64MB.
Monitor	Super VGA monitor with 800×600 resolution.

Before you install IIS 4.0, remove any installations of a previous version of IIS. You'll also need to disable other versions of FTP, Gopher, or World Wide Web services you have installed under Windows NT Server 4.0. This includes the Windows Academic Center (EMWAC) service included with the Windows NT Resource Kit.

You also should have the following software installed:

◆ Windows NT Server 4.0

◆ Service Pack 3 for Windows NT Server 4.0

◆ Internet Explorer (4.01 or later).

You also must be logged on to the Windows NT Server computer with Administrator privileges. Failing to have proper permissions or the required software installed will almost always guarantee a failed installation.

TCP/IP Problems

Three main parameters specify how TCP/IP is configured on a host with the ability to communicate beyond its network ID: the IP address, the subnet mask, and the default gateway, which is the address of the router.

DHCP Client Configuration Problems

Using a DHCP server can greatly reduce TCP/IP configuration problems. If the DHCP scope is set up properly, without any typos or other configuration errors, DHCP clients shouldn't have any configuration problems. It is impossible to completely eliminate human error, but using DHCP should reduce the points of potential errors to just the DHCP servers rather than every client on the network.

Even when there are no configuration problems with DHCP addresses, DHCP clients can get a duplicate IP address from a DHCP server. If you have multiple DHCP servers in your environment, you should have scopes on each DHCP server for different subnets. Usually you have scopes with a larger number of addresses for the local subnet where the DHCP server is located and smaller scopes for other subnets. Creating multiple scopes on one server provides backup for giving clients IP addresses. If the server on the local scope is busy or down, the client can still receive an address from a remote DHCP server. When the router forwards this DHCP request to another subnet's server, it includes the address of the subnet it came from so that the remote DHCP server knows from which subnet scope of addresses to lease an address to the remote client. Using this type of redundancy, however, can cause problems if you don't configure the scopes on all the DHCP servers correctly.

The most important part of the configuration is to make sure you don't have duplicate addresses in the different scopes. On one server, for example, you could have a scope in the range 131.107.2.100 to 131.107.2.170. On the remote DHCP server, you could have a scope of 131.107.2.171 to 131.107.2.200. By setting up the scopes without overlap, you should not have any problems with clients receiving duplicate IP addresses. DHCP servers do not communicate with each other, so one server does not know anything about the addresses the other server has leased. Therefore, you must ensure the servers never give out duplicate information by making sure the scopes for one subnet on all the different DHCP servers have unique IP addresses.

RESOLVING SECURITY PROBLEMS

Security problems relate to a user or users being unable to utilize the resources you have made available to them or too many users being able to access what only one or two should be able to access. There is an unlimited number of reasons why these things could happen, based on what the resources are and how they are accessed.

Problem Areas

A number of different problem areas are examined below through the presentation of various issues involving server technologies.

In most Web server operations, you want to make the service available to the public, and to as many users as possible. Unfortunately, this can lead to the risk of letting in unwanted traffic, as well. Solutions to solving this problem are: using a firewall to restrict traffic, disabling anonymous usage, and/or moving the Web server service to a port other than its default 80—essentially hiding it from the outside world (discussed in more detail in the section on resolving WWW service problems).

- Firewalls can be used to restrict incoming traffic to only those services you are choosing to allow in. Additionally, a firewall can be used to prevent all traffic from coming in. If you are attempting to make data available on the Web, consider putting the Web server outside the firewall and allowing traffic to pass to it but to nothing else on your network.

- Anonymous usage is a staple of most public Web sites. If you do not want to have a public Web site, however, consider disabling the logon. You can configure the Web server to use user authentication to verify that everyone accessing it has a valid Windows NT user account (and they must give a username and password before being allowed to interact with the server).

- Secure Sockets Layer (SSL) 3.0 is included with IIS and its use should be mandatory on any site holding sensitive data (such as medical information, credit card information, and so on). SSL allows a secure connection to be established between the browser and the server, and encryption can be used between them.

- Server Certificates, a part of SSL, can be created (unique digital identifications) to authenticate your Web site to browsers. This is used for public and private key (key pair) interactions of a secure nature.

- NTFS permissions can be used in conjunction with IIS to secure individual files and directories from those who should not access them. The five permission types are:

  - Change—users can read and modify files, including deleting them and adding new ones to a directory

  - Full Control—the default for the Everyone group—users can modify, move, delete, take ownership, and even change permissions

  - No Access—overrides everything else and gives absolutely no access to the resource

  - Read—as the name implies, users can read the data

  - Special Access—users permissions have been set to something specific by the administrator

Far and away, the No Access permission is the most powerful permission. When it is implemented, the user that has been assigned this permission will have no access to that resource. It does not matter what other permissions have been assigned. The No Access permission will override any other assigned permissions.

Following the Basic Steps in the Access Control Process

Solving most security problems involves using a great deal of common sense (if passwords are used, make them more than one character in length, and so on) and understanding what is taking place. The following steps illustrate the access control process:

1. The Web server receives a request from the browser to perform an operation.

2. The Web server checks to see whether the IP address is permitted. If there are no restrictions on IP address ranges, or the request is coming from a valid range, processing continues.

3. The Web server checks to see whether the user is permitted.

4. The Web server checks to see if its own permissions will allow access.

5. A check is made to see whether the NTFS permissions will allow access.

If any of the steps above fails, the access is denied. If they all succeed, access is granted.

RESOLVING RESOURCE ACCESS PROBLEMS

A user or users who are unable to access a resource identify resource access problems. A lack of appropriate security or the TCP/IP configuration of the host can cause this problem for clients.

Using IPCONFIG to Resolve DHCP Address Problems

When a DHCP client gets an IP that is not configured correctly or if the client doesn't get an IP address at all, IPCONFIG can be used to resolve these problems. If the client gets incorrect IP parameters, it should be apparent from the results of IPCONFIG /all. You should be able to see that some of the parameters don't match the IP address or that some parameters are completely blank. For example, you could have the wrong default gateway (in which case the entry would not appear), or the client might not be configured to be a WINS client.

When a DHCP client fails to receive an address, the results of IPCONFIG /all are different. In this case, the client has an IP address of 0.0.0.0—an invalid address—and the DHCP server is 255.255.255.255—a broadcast address.

To fix this problem, you can release the incorrect address with IPCONFIG /release and then try to obtain a new IP address with IPCONFIG /renew. The IPCONFIG /renew command sends out a new request for a DHCP address. If a DHCP server is available, the server responds with the lease of an IP address. If there is no response, it sends a request for a new one.

In many cases, the DHCP client will acquire the same address after releasing and renewing. That the client receives the same address indicates the same DHCP server responded to the renewal request and gave out the address that had just been released back into the pool of available addresses. If you need to renew an address because the parameters of the scope are incorrect, you must fix the parameters in DHCP configuration before releasing and renewing the address. Otherwise, the client could receive the same address again with the same incorrect parameters.

Diagnosing and Resolving Name Resolution Problems

Name resolution problems are easily identified as such with the PING utility. If you can ping a host using its IP address but cannot ping it by its host name, you have a resolution problem. If you cannot ping the host at all, the problem lies elsewhere.

Problems that can occur with name resolution and their solutions fit into the following categories:

+ The entry is misspelled. Examine the HOSTS or LMHOSTS file to verify that the host name is correctly spelled. If you are using the HOSTS file on a system prior to Windows NT 4.0, capitalization is important because this file is case sensitive, whereas LMHOSTS is not case sensitive (regardless of the Windows NT version number).

+ Comment characters prevent the entry from being read. Verify that a pound sign is not at the beginning of the line (with the exception of entries such as #PRE and #DOM in LMHOSTS only), or anywhere on the line prior to the host name.

+ There are duplicate entries in the file. Because the files are read in linear fashion, with any duplication, only the first entry is read and all others are ignored. Verify that all host names are unique.

+ A host other than the one you want is contacted. Verify that the IP address entered in the file(s) is valid and corresponds to the host name.

- The wrong file is used. While similar in nature, HOSTS and LMHOSTS are really quite different, and not all that interchangeable. HOSTS is used to map IP addresses to host names, and LMHOSTS is used to map NetBIOS names to IP addresses.

RESOLVING INDEX SERVER PROBLEMS

Index Server works with IIS through queries that come in the form of .idq (Internet Data Query) files. It responds to those queries in the form of .idq files as well. In order to function properly, .idq files should always be placed in the Scripts directory, and they require Execute or Script permission.

As discussed in Chapter 4, "Integration and Interoperability," there are two sections to .idq files with [Query] being required, and [Names] being optional (used only to define nonstandard column names that are referred to in a query). Refer to Chapter 5 for a listing of parameters, variables, and conditional expressions.

Most troubleshooting/trouble correction is implemented automatically with Index Server. For example, if the cache becomes corrupted, Index Server will begin a recovery operation, and no administrator interaction is required. In all events, messages are written to the event log indicating the actions taking place, and administrators can monitor their Index Server from there.

Query Errors

Errors can, and often do, occur when improper syntax is used in queries. There are a series of standard messages returned to alert you that this is the cause of the problem, and this section examines those.

Syntax Errors

According to Microsoft's online documentation (ixerrysn.htm), the error messages in Table 7.3 can be returned when executing a query.

TABLE 7.3

THE IXERRYSN.HTM FILE

Message	Explanation
Expecting closing parenthesis ')'.	Occurs when parentheses are mismatched.
Expecting closing square bracket ']'.	An opening square bracket was not followed by a closing square bracket. Usually the result of an ill-formed weight.
Expecting comma.	Occurs when a reserved token or end-of-string occurs before the closing brace of a vector property. Example: @VectorString = {A1, B@}.
Expecting currency.	A currency value was expected but not found. Occurs when a property of type DBTYPE_CY is fed incorrect input. Correct format for currency is #.#.
Expecting date.	A date was expected but not found. Occurs when a property of type DBTYPE_DATE is fed incorrect input. Allowed formats for dates are *yyyy/mm/dd, yyyy/mm/dd hh:mm:ss,* and relative dates *(-#y, -#m, -#w, -#d, -#h, -#n, -#s)*.
Expecting end of string.	A complete restriction has been parsed, and there is still more input. Example: (@size = 100).
Expecting GUID.	A GUID (Globally Unique Identifier) was expected but not found. Occurs when a property of DBTYPE_GUID is fed incorrect input. Property format for a GUID is *XXXXXXXX-XXXX-XXXX-XXXX-XXXXXXXXXXXX.*
Expecting integer.	An integer was expected but not found. Occurs when a property of an integer type (DBTYPE_I4, and so on) is fed a nonnumeric value, or a nonnumeric vector weight is entered.
Expecting phrase.	A textual phrase was expected and not found. This error occurs in a variety of situations where the query parser is expecting plain text and is given a special token instead.
Expecting property name.	Occurs when a correctly formed property name is not found after an @ sign.
Expecting real number.	A real number was expected but not found. Occurs when a property of a real type (DBTYPE_R4, and so on) is fed a nonnumeric value.

Message	*Explanation*
Expecting regular expression.	Similar to Expecting phrase error. Used when in regular-expression parsing mode.
The file <file> is on a remote UNC share. .Idq, ida, and .htx files cannot be placed on a remote UNC share.	An .idq, .ida, or .htx file was found on a remote UNC share. None of these files can be on a remote UNC share.
Invalid literal.	Occurs only when a query property is formatted poorly. Almost all conditions are covered by the Expecting Integer, Expecting Date, and other errors.
No such property.	Property specified after @, #, or $ does not exist. It is not a default property and is not specified in the [Names] section of the .idq file.
Not yet implemented.	An unimplemented feature of Index Server.
Out of memory.	The server ran out of memory processing the CiRestriction.
Regular expressions require a property of type string.	A property of a nontextual type (DBTYPE_I4, DBTYPE_GUID, and so on) was selected for regular-expression mode. For example, #size 100* will cause this error.
Unexpected end of string.	There is a missing quotation mark in your query.
Unsupported property type.	For future expansion. Will occur when a display-only property type is used in a query restriction.
Weight must be between 0 and 1000.	Occurs when a query term weight is outside the legal range of 0 to 1000.

IDQ File Errors

According to Microsoft's online documentation in file ixerridq.htm, the messages in Table 7.4 are returned by use of the CiErrorMessage variable, accessible from .htx error pages.

TABLE 7.4

THE IXERRIDQ.HTM FILE

Message	Explanation
The catalog directory cannot be found in the location specified by 'CiCatalog=' in file *<file>*.	The catalog location specified by the CiCatalog parameter did not contain a valid content index catalog.
DBTYPE_BYREF must be used with DBTYPE_STR, DBTYPE_WSTR, DBTYPE_GUID or DBTYPE_UI1 types.	DBTYPE_BYREF must always be used in conjunction with an indirect type in the [Names] section.
DBTYPE_VECTOR or DBTYPE_BYREF used alone.	The VECTOR and BYREF property modifiers must always be used with a type. Example: DBTYPE_I4 ¦ DBTYPE_VECTOR
Duplicate column, possibly by a column alias, found in the 'CiColumns=' specification in file *<file>*.	The same property was named more than once in the CiColumns line. It may have been mentioned with different friendly names that refer to the same property.
Duplicate property name.	The same property was defined twice in the [Names] section.
Expecting closing parenthesis.	Opening parenthesis in [Names] section is not followed by closing parenthesis in .idq file.
Expecting GUID.	Incorrectly formatted entry in the [Names] section of the .idq file.
Expecting integer.	Incorrectly formatted entry in the [Names] section of the .idq file.
Expecting property name.	Incorrectly formatted entry in the [Names] section of .idq file.
Expecting property specifier.	Invalid or missing property specifier in [Names] section. Property is named either by PROPID (integer) or string.
Expecting SHALLOW or DEEP in .idq file *<file>* on line 'CiFlags='.	The CiFlags parameter has a value other than SHALLOW or DEEP.
Expecting TRUE or FALSE in .idq file *<file>* on line 'CiForceUseCi='.	The CiForceUseCi parameter has a value other than TRUE or FALSE.

Message	*Explanation*
Expecting type specifier.	Incorrectly formatted entry in the [Names] section of .idq file.
Failed to set property name.	A resource failure. Usually out-of-memory.
The file `<file>` is on a network share. IDQ, IDA, and HTX files cannot be placed on a network share.	You must put these files into a virtual root on the local computer.
The .htx file specified could not be found in any virtual or physical path.	The file specified in the CiTemplate parameter could not be located.
The IDQ file `<file>` contains a duplicate entry on line `<line>`.	A parameter in the [Query] section of the .idq file was given more than once.
The IDQ file `<file>` could not be found.	Check the path to the .idq file and then make sure the .idq file is in that path.
An invalid 'CiScope=' or 'CiCatalog=' was specified in file `<file>`.	The .idq file cannot contain invalid parameters. Correct the condition and try again.
Invalid GUID.	A poorly formatted GUID was found in the [Names] section.
An invalid locale was specified on the 'CiLocale=' line in .idq file `<file>`.	The locale ID specified by the CiLocale parameter was not recognized as a valid locale ID.
Invalid property found in the 'CiColumns=' specification in file `<file>`.	A property specified in the CiColumns parameter is not a standard property and is not listed in the [Names] section of the .idq file.
Invalid property found in the 'CiSort=' specification in file `<file>`.	A property specified in the CiSort parameter is not a standard property and is not listed in the [Names] section of the .idq file.
An invalid sort order was specified on the 'CiSort=' line in file `<file>`. Only [a] and [d] are supported.	A sort-order specification following a property name in the CiSort parameter was unrecognized. Only [a] (for ascending) and [d] (for descending) are allowed.

continues

TABLE 7.4 continued

Message	*Explanation*
One or more output columns must be specified in the .idq file <file>.	The CiColumns parameter is missing or empty. At least one output column must be specified for the query.
Operation on line number of IDA file file is invalid.	An unrecognized keyword was found in the .ida file.
The query failed because the Web server is busy processing other requests.	The limit on the number of queries has been exceeded. To allow more queries to wait in the queue for processing, increase the value of the Registry key IsapiRequestQueueSize, and to allow more queries to be processed simultaneously, increase the value for the Registry key IsapiRequestThresholdFactor.
Read error in file <file>.	I/O error occurred reading the file. Generally caused by hardware failure.
A restriction must be specified in the .idq file <file>.	The CiRestriction parameter is missing or empty. Every query must have a restriction. A restriction such as #vpath *.* will match all pages.
A scope must be specified in the .idq file <file>.	The CiScope parameter is missing or empty. Every query must have a scope. The scope / (forward slash) will match every page in all virtual directories and the scope \ (backslash) will match every page on every physical path.
The template file cannot be found in the location specified by 'CiTemplate=' in file <file>.	An attempt to open an .htx file at the location specified by the CiTemplate parameter failed. The path may be invalid, it may specify a directory, or it may resolve to NULL after parameter replacement.
A template file must be specified in the .idq file <file>.	The CiTemplate parameter is missing or empty. Every query must have a template (.htx) file.
Template for IDA file file cannot have detail section.	A <%BeginDetail%> was found in the .ida file. Please remove it and the entire detail section.

Message	Explanation
Unrecognized type.	Type specified is not one of the valid types (DBTYPE_I4, DBTYPE_GUID, and so on).
You must specify 'MaxRecordsPerPage' in the .idq file <file>.	The CiMaxRecordsPerPage parameter is missing or empty. Every query must specify the number of records per page.

Event Log Messages

Index Server system errors are reported in the application event log under the Ci Filter Service category. System errors reported here include page filtering (indexing) problems, out-of-resource conditions, index corruption, and so on.

The messages in Table 7.5 are written to the Windows NT application event log. This is from Microsoft's online documentation (ixerrlog.htm).

TABLE 7.5

THE IXERRLOG.HTM FILE

Message	Explanation
Account *user-id* does not have interactive logon privilege on this computer. You can give *user-id* interactive logon privilege on this computer using the user manager administrative tool.	The specified *user-id* does not have interactive logon privilege on the computer running Index Server. Give the *user-id* interactive logon privilege through the User Manager for Domains.
The CI filter daemon has prematurely stopped and will be subsequently restarted.	The filter daemon (Cidaemon.exe) stopped unexpectedly. It will be automatically restarted. This can be caused by poorly written filters, or experimentation with the Windows NT Task Manager.
CI has started on <catalog>.	An informational message logged when Index Server is started successfully.

continues

TABLE **7.5**   **continued**

Message	*Explanation*
`Class for extension <extension> unknown. Sample file: <file>.`	This is a warning that files with the specified extension are being filtered with the default (text) filter. This can lead to addition of unnecessary data in the index. Consider turning off filtering for this extension. The full physical path of a representative file is included in the message. Generation of this message can be disabled by turning on a special flag in `ContentIndex` Registry key.
`Cleaning up corrupted content index metadata on <catalog>. Index will be automatically restored by refiltering all documents.`	A catastrophic data corruption error was detected on the specified catalog. The catalog will be rebuilt. This is usually caused by hardware failure, but can also occur in rare circumstances because of abrupt shutdown or power failure. Recovery will occur automatically.
`Content index on <catalog> could not be initialized. Error <number>.`	Unknown, possibly catastrophic error. Please report the error number to Microsoft Technical Support. To recover, delete all files under *<catalog>* and re-index.
`Content index on <catalog> is corrupted. Please shut down and restart Web server.`	A catastrophic data corruption error was detected on the specified catalog. The catalog will be rebuilt. This is usually caused by hardware failure, but can also occur in rare circumstances because of abrupt shutdown or power failure. You must shut down and restart the Web server for recovery to occur.

Message	*Explanation*
Content index corruption detected in component `<component>`. Stack trace is `<stack>`.	The content index is corrupted. Delete the catalog and start over. If you keep getting this error, remove and reinstall Index Server.
Content index corruption detected in component `<component>` in catalog `<catalog>`. Stack trace is `<stack>`.	The content index is corrupt. Delete the catalog and start over. If you keep getting this error, remove and reinstall Index Server.
The content index could not filter file `<file>`. The filter operation was retried `<number>` times without success.	The specified document failed to successfully filter *<number>* times. This usually indicates a corrupted document or corrupted properties. In rare cases, filtering may fail because the document was in use for a long period of time.
Content index on drive is corrupted. Please shut down and restart the Content Index service (cisvc).	In the Windows NT Control Panel under Services, stop the Content Index service, and then restart it.
The content index filter for file "`<file>`" generated content data more than `<size>` times the file's size.	Filtering of the specified document generated more than the allowed maximum amount of output. This is usually caused by a poorly written filter, a corrupted document, or both.
The content index filter stopped while filtering "`<file>`". The CI daemon was restarted. Please check the validity of the filter for objects of this class.	Filtering of the specified document was started, but did not finish before the timeout period expired. This is usually caused by a poorly written filter, a corrupted document, or both.
A content scan has completed on `<catalog>`.	A content scan of the catalog has been completed successfully.
An error has been detected on `<catalog>` that requires a full content scan.	The catalog lost a change notification, usually due to lack of resources (disk space) or hardware failure. The complete scope of the catalog will be scanned, and all documents will be refiltered. This action is deferred until a suitable time.

continues

TABLE 7.5   continued

Message	*Explanation*
An error has been detected in content index on `<catalog>`.	The content index is corrupt. Delete the catalog and start over. If you keep getting this error, remove and reinstall Index Server.
An error has been detected on `<catalog>` that requires a partial content scan.	The catalog lost a change notification, usually due to lack of resources (disk space) or hardware failure. A partial scope of the catalog will be scanned, and some documents will be refiltered. This action is deferred until a suitable time.
Error `<number>` detected in content index on `<catalog>`.	Unknown, possibly catastrophic error. Please report error number to Microsoft Technical Support. To recover, delete all files under *<catalog>* and start over.
File change notifications are turned off for scope "`<scope>`" because of error `<number>`. This scope will be periodically rescanned.	An error prevented re-establishing automatic change notifications for the specified directory scope. To determine documents that changed in the scope, periodic incremental scans will be done by Index Server. The rescan interval is specified in the Registry.
File change notifications for scope "`<scope>`" are not enabled because of error `<number>`. This scope will be periodically rescanned.	An error prevented establishment of automatic change notifications for the specified directory scope. This usually happens with virtual roots that point to remote shares on file servers that do not support automatic change notifications. To determine which documents changed in the scope, periodic incremental scans will be done by Index Server. The rescan interval is specified in the Registry.

Message	*Explanation*
The filter service could not run since file `<file>` could not be found on your system.	An executable or DLL required for filtering cannot be found, usually because Cidaemon.exe is not on the path.
A full content scan has started on `<catalog>`.	A complete rescan of the catalog has been initiated.
`<number>` inconsistencies were detected in PropertyStore during recovery of catalog `<catalog>`.	Corruption was detected in the property cache during startup. Recovery is automatically scheduled. Usually the result of hardware failure or abrupt shutdown.
Master merge cannot be restarted on `<catalog>` due to error `<number>`.	A master merge cannot be restarted on the specified catalog. The error code gives the reason.
Master merge cannot be started on `<catalog>` due to error `<number>`.	A master merge cannot be started on the specified catalog. The error code gives the reason.
Master merge has been paused on `<catalog>`. It will be rescheduled later.	A master merge has been temporarily halted on the specified catalog. Often occurs when a merge runs out of system resources (disk space, memory, and so on).
Master merge has completed on `<catalog>`.	A master merge has been completed on the specified catalog. This is an informational message.
Master merge has restarted on `<catalog>`.	A paused master merge has been restarted.
Master merge has started on `<catalog>`.	A master merge has been initiated on the specified catalog. This is an informational message.
Master merge was started on `<catalog>` because the amount of remaining disk space was less than `<number>`%.	A master merge was started because the amount of free space on the catalog volume dropped below a minimum threshold. The total free disk space should be increased after the master merge completes.

continues

TABLE 7.5 continued

Message	*Explanation*
Master merge was started on `<catalog>` because more than `<number>` documents have changed since the last master merge.	A master merge was started because the number of documents changed since the last master merge exceeded the maximum threshold.
Master merge was started on `<catalog>` because the size of the shadow indexes is more than `<number>`% the disk.	A master merge was started because the amount of data in shadow indexes exceeded the maximum threshold.
Notifications are not enabled on `<pathname>` because this is a DFS aware share. This scope will be periodically scanned.	If a virtual root points to a distributed file system (DFS) share, notifications are disabled for the entire DFS share because DFS does not support notifications.
One or more embeddings in file `<file>` could not be filtered.	The specified file was filtered correctly, but several of the embedded objects could not be filtered. This is usually caused by embedded objects without a registered filter. Text within unfiltered embedded objects is not searchable. Generation of this message can be disabled by turning on a special flag in key Registry.
The path `<pathname>` is too long for Content Index.	The Content Index service detected a path that was longer than the maximum number of characters allowed for a pathname as determined by the constant MAX_PATH (260 characters). As a result, no documents from that path will be returned or indexed.
Please check your system time. It might be set to an invalid value.	This event is generated when the system time is invalid, for example, when set to a date before January 1, 1980. When the system time is invalid, the date may appear as 2096.

Message	*Explanation*
`<Process-Name> failed to logon <UserId> because of error <number>.`	The specified process (Index Server SearchEngine or CiDaemon) failed to log on the specified user because of an error. The remote shares for which the UserId is used will not be filtered correctly. This can happen if either the password is wrong or the validity of the password could not be verified due to network errors.
`PropertyStore inconsistency detected in catalog <catalog>.`	Corruption was detected in the property cache. Recovery is automatically scheduled. Usually the result of hardware failure or abrupt shutdown.
`Recovery is starting on PropertyStore in catalog <catalog>.`	Corruption was detected in the property cache. Recovery is starting on the property cache. This can take a long time depending on the size of the property cache.
`Recovery was performed successfully on PropertyStore in catalog <catalog>.`	Corruption was detected in the property cache. The error has been fixed. Usually the result of hardware failure or abrupt shutdown.
`Very low disk space was detected on drive <drive>. Please free up at least <number> MB of space for content index to continue.`	Free space has fallen below the minimum threshold required for successful merge. This is just a warning, but no merges will be initiated until space is freed up. Filtering will also stop.

Virtual Roots

Table 7.6, which follows, is from the ixerrlog.htm as well, and describes the error messages that occur when virtual root problems are the cause of the error.

TABLE 7.6

THE VIRTUAL ROOTS COMPONENT OF IXERRLOG.HTM

Message	Explanation
Added virtual root <root> to index.	The message "Mapped to *<path>*" is added to the event log when a virtual root is indexed.
Removed virtual root <root> from index.	This message is written to the event log when a virtual root is deleted from the index.
Added scope <path> to index.	This message is added to the event log when a new physical scope is indexed.
Removed scope <path> from index.	This message is written to the event log when a new physical scope is deleted from the index.

Other Index Server Issues

Other issues to be aware of with Index Server include:

- Index Server starting and stopping
- Word weighting
- Disk filling

Index Server Starting and Stopping

Index Server, by default, is set to automatically start when IIS does. If this is set to another value, such as manual, IIS can be started from the Services icon in the Control Panel. This is the same utility that can be used to stop the Index Server service, although it will automatically shut down when IIS does.

If Index Server is not running and a query comes in, Index Server will automatically start. Therefore, as an administrator, starting Index Server manually is not something you should ever need to do. As an administrator, the stopping of Index Server is something you should never need to do, either, but you can do it from the Services utility.

Word Weighting

Word weighting determines how words in the data are indexed. This process is done by the Waisindx.exe utility. It determines what to index, how much to weight words, how to optimize the server, and where to find the actual data. As a rule of thumb, seven indexes are created for each data file, with the combined size of the seven indexes being equal to 110% of the size of the data file.

The weighting factors that Waisindx.exe uses are as follows:

- The actual weight of the word as to whether it appears in a headline, capitalized, and so on, or just in the body of the data.

- The term of the weight—how many times does it appear, and thus, how important is it to the data.

- The proximity—how close two multiple words always appear to each other. For example, "computer publishing".

- The density of the word. This is computed by taking the number of times the word appears and dividing it by the total number of all words in the data.

When Waisindx.exe is run, it creates the indexes that are then used to locate the data. As you add new records to the data, the indexes are not updated, and you must rerun Waisindx.exe to create new indexes incorporating the new data.

Running Out of Disk Space

One of the most common problems with using Index Server is running out of disk space. If the drive fills, indexing is paused, and the only method of knowing this is by a message written to the event log. The event log should be monitored routinely by an administrator for this and similar occurrences.

RESOLVING SETUP ISSUES WHEN INSTALLING IIS ON A WINDOWS NT SERVER 4.0 COMPUTER

As discussed earlier in this chapter, before you install IIS 4.0, you must remove any installations of a previous version of IIS, and disable other versions of FTP, Gopher, or World Wide Web services running under Windows NT Server 4.0.

You must be logged on to the Windows NT Server computer with Administrator privileges, and need to have the following software installed:

◆ Windows NT Server 4.0

◆ Service Pack 3 for Windows NT Server 4.0

◆ Internet Explorer (4.01 or higher)

If all of the preceding conditions have been met, and problems exist, you should know where to turn for assistance. There are a number of places to find help, and they include:

◆ The Windows NT Resource Kit

◆ Online help in both Windows NT and IIS

◆ Microsoft Technet

◆ CompuServe

◆ The Microsoft Internet site

The Microsoft Windows NT Resource Kit includes three volumes of in-depth information and a CD of utilities. The Resource Kit utilities add a large number of troubleshooting utilities and can help you isolate problems much easier.

The online help in Windows NT is available from the Start Menu, Help, or from almost anywhere else in the product by pressing F1. The IIS help is available at several locations, but most notably by selecting Product Documentation from the IIS section of the Programs menu.

Microsoft Technet is a monthly CD subscription that includes the latest service packs, drivers, and updates for all operating system products. Once installed, you can run it at any time by choosing Microsoft Technet from the Programs menu.

The CompuServe forums are not as well supported as they once were and almost everything is shifting to the Web, but they are still a good location to find interaction among users experiencing similar problems. The easiest method of finding a forum supporting the problem you are experiencing is to click on the stoplight icon on the main CompuServe menu (or at a command prompt, type **GO**) and enter NDEX. This will bring up an index of all the forums currently available. You can select a choice from the list, or—depending on your version of CompuServe— choose GO again, and enter the abbreviation for the forum you want.

The Microsoft Internet site at `http://www.microsoft.com/support` makes available all software updates and patches. It also serves as an entry point to the KnowledgeBase where you can find documentation on all known problems. You can also check the public news servers at `MSNEWS.Microsoft.com`.

USE A WEBMAP TO FIND AND REPAIR BROKEN LINKS, HYPERLINK TEXTS, HEADINGS, AND TITLES

Content Analyzer's WebMaps can be used to administer Web site content to help you keep your Web site up to date and functioning correctly. Use the Link Info window, searches, and properties to help you manage your site's content. In this section you are shown how to use the Link Info windows to find and repair the following:

- Broken links
- Hyperlink text
- Headings
- Titles

To show the Link Info window, create a WebMap of your Web site. Click the Object Links toolbar button, or right-click the page you want to view and select Links. The Link Info window displays (see Figure 7.1). In this window, you can display different types of links on a page.

Click the Links on Page option to display all links on a selected page. This is handy if you want to review navigational paths on a page.

Click the InLinks option to display links that reference the page you are reviewing. These are called InLinks, and can be from pages on the same site as the page you're viewing or from another site.

When you click the Main Route option, the Link Info window displays all ancestor links from the main page to the selected page. If the page you're reviewing is your site's home page, for instance, you will not see any other ancestors. However, if the page is one level below the home page (that is, you can link to the page from the home page), you'll see the home page displayed when selecting the Main Route option. This is because the home page is the *parent* of the page you're reviewing. Pages one level below the child page are considered *grandchildren* to the home page, and so on. You'll find this option handy when you're viewing a page that is buried deep in the hierarchy and ancestry is not easy to discern.

Finally, to see the number of links for each type of link option you can display, look at the bottom of the Link Info window.

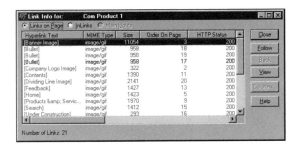

FIGURE 7.1
The Link Info window.

Fix Broken Links

As your Web site matures and content is upgraded, deleted, moved, and renamed, you'll need to update links on your pages. Over time, however, some of your page may contain broken links, those references that lead nowhere. You can use a WebMap to discover broken links and then launch your Web page editor to fix the link.

You can use two methods to search for broken objects in your pages. One way is to conduct a search for all links that are broken. Another way is to search for broken objects or for objects based on a specific HTTP status.

To search for broken links, use these steps:

1. Create a WebMap and select Tools, Custom Search (or click the Search toolbar button). The Search dialog box displays.

2. Configure the Search dialog box using the following parameters:

    *   Object Type set to Links

    *   Field set to Broken

    *   Modifiers set to Equals

    *   Value set to True

> **NOTE**
>
> There is also an option to select TOOLS, QUICK SEARCH and BROKEN LINKS.

3. Click Search. The Search Results window displays all broken links, if any.

Sometimes links are shown as broken (shown in red) but really are not. An example is a site that is unavailable because of repairs it is going through. Or, there is too much network traffic to enable you to connect to the server. You may need to try the site later to establish a connection to it.

To fix a broken link from the Search Results window, do the following:

1. Select the link.

2. Select the parent page (the page that includes the broken link) of the page you just selected.

3. Select Tools, Launch Helper App.

Checking and Modifying Hyperlink Text

Text that is used to describe a link (that is, the text that is hyperlinked to another object) also can be viewed using the Content Analyzer. Many sites like to use consistent wording and spellings for hyperlink text pointing to the same object. You can check the InLinks text to a particular object quickly with Content Analyzer. Then, if necessary, launch your editor to modify this text.

To review the hyperlink text, use these steps:

1. Select the object that you want to see the InLinks text for.

2. Click the Object Links toolbar button. The Link Info window displays.

3. Click the InLinks option.

4. Scroll through the list of InLinks and view the hyperlink text in the Hyperlink Text column.

5. Select a link you want to change and click Follow. The page you want to change displays.

6. Right-click a page you want to modify and select Launch Helper App and the specific application to modify the page. Change the hyperlink text on that page.

If Hyperlink Text is not a column in the Links Info window, add it by right-clicking any column header in the Links Info window. Use the Configure Columns dialog box to add the Hyperlink Text column to the Links Info window. Click Done.

Checking and Changing Headers

Content Analyzer can be used to check header information in pages. Headers are HTML tags used to set up sections in your Web pages.

To view headers on a page in Content Analyzer, do the following:

1. Create a WebMap.

2. Right-click a page you want to check.

3. Select Properties to display the Properties dialog box.

4. Click the Page tab and review the Headings area.

5. Click OK to close the Properties dialog box.

If the page you just checked includes a header you want to change, or does not include headers but you want to add them to the page, right-click the page in the WebMap and select Launch Helper App. Select the helper application that enables you to edit the source code of the page. Modify the page to include headers.

Checking Page Titles

You can use Content Analyzer to check page titles. Page titles are referenced by many index servers, as well as used by some browsers (such as Internet Explorer) in bookmark lists.

You'll probably want to check page titles as your Web page content changes or evolves. To check page titles, perform these steps:

1. Create a WebMap and perform a Custom Search for all pages.

2. Add the Title column to the Search Results window. This shows you the titles for each page displayed.

3. Double-click an object in the Search Results window. The associated browser launches, with the page displayed. Review the page to see if the title for it describes the content of the page. If a title is not shown, create a title for the page based on its content. You can then launch a helper application for editing Web pages to add or modify a page's title.

RESOLVING WWW SERVICE PROBLEMS

HTTP is currently the most used protocol on the Internet. The default control port assignment is 80, and you can "hide" the service by moving it to any other available port above 1023.

By default, all configured IIS services (WWW, FTP, and so on) start and stop automatically when IIS does. You can start, stop, or pause it by site by following these steps:

1. Start Internet Service Manager, and select the site.

2. Right-click the mouse and choose which of the three options you want (Start, Stop, or Pause).

3. Alternatively, after selecting the site, you can choose the action to take from the toolbar.

If users experience problems viewing your Web site, it can be an indication of permission problems. Make certain that Read permission is assigned to all users for the directory containing the site.

The Anonymous Access and Authentication Control field of the site's property sheet will allow you to choose among anonymous access, basic authentication permissions, or Windows NT Challenge/Response. Work backwards in selecting an option from the list until you hit the combination allowing all of your clients to connect to the site without difficulty.

RESOLVING FTP SERVICE PROBLEMS

As discussed elsewhere in this book, you can install a Windows NT FTP server that can provide FTP file transfer services to other systems. This allows the server to serve clients in the same manner that has been traditionally done on UNIX machines. The FTP service is a component of IIS.

FTP, or file transfer protocol, provides a simple but robust mechanism for copying files to or from remote hosts using the connection-oriented services of TCP/IP. FTP is a component of the TCP/IP protocol, and is defined in RFC 959. To use FTP to send or receive files, the following requirements must be met:

- ◆ The client computer must have FTP client software, such as the FTP client included with Windows NT.

- ◆ The user must have a username and password on the remote system. In some cases, a username of *anonymous* with no password suffices.

- ◆ The remote system must be running an FTP daemon or service (depending upon whether it is UNIX or NT).

- ◆ Your system and the remote system must be running the TCP/IP protocol.

You can use FTP in either a command line mode or in a command interpreter mode. The following options are available from the command line:

```
C:\>ftp ?
Transfers files to and from a computer running an FTP server service
(sometimes called a daemon). FTP can be used interactively.

FTP [-v] [-d] [-i] [-n] [-g] [-s:filename] [-a] [-w:windowsize]
[host]

      -v            Suppresses display of remote server responses.
      -n            Suppresses auto-login upon initial connection.
      -i            Turns off interactive prompting during multiple
                    file transfers.
      -d            Enables debugging.
      -g            Disables filename globbing (see GLOB command).
      -s:filename   Specifies a text file containing FTP commands; the
                    commands will automatically run after FTP starts.
      -a            Use any local interface when binding data
                    connection.
      -w:buffersize Overrides the default transfer buffer size of 4096.
      host          Specifies the host name or IP address of the remote
                    host to connect to.
```

If you use FTP in a command interpreter mode, some of the more frequently used options are as follows:

- ◆ open—Specifies the remote system to which you connect.

- ◆ close—Disconnects from a remote system. Bye or Quit work as well.

- ◆ ls—Obtains a directory listing on a remote system, much like the dir command in DOS. Note that the ls -1 command provides file size and time stamps. In Windows NT you can use the old DOS "DIR" as well.

- cd—Changes directories on the remote system. This command functions in much the same way as the DOS cd command.

- lcd—Changes directories on the local system. This command also functions in much the same way as the DOS cd command.

- binary—Instructs FTP to treat all files transferred as binary.

- ascii—Instructs FTP to treat all files transferred as text. The need to choose a transfer type is that certain files cannot be read correctly as binary, while ASCII is universally accepted.

- get—Copies a file from the remote host to your local computer.

- put—Copies a file from your local computer to the remote host.

- debug—Turns on debugging commands that can be useful in diagnosing problems.

Because remote host systems typically are based on UNIX, you will encounter a number of nuances relating to UNIX if you interact with these hosts in your FTP connections, such as the following:

- The UNIX operating system uses the forward slash in path references, not the backward slash. In UNIX, the file name \WINNT40\README.TXT would be /WINNT40 /README.TXT.

- UNIX is case sensitive at all times—the command get MyFile and the command get MYFILE are not the same. Usernames and passwords are also case sensitive.

- UNIX treats wild card characters, such as the asterisk and the question mark, differently. The glob command within FTP changes how wild card characters in local filenames are treated.

The biggest problems with FTP typically involve permissions in uploading and downloading files. To upload files, a user (whether specified by name or anonymous) must have change permission to the directory. To download files, a user (again, either by name or anonymous) must have read permission. These represent the very bare-bones permissions required to perform these operations. If an anonymous user cannot get connected, verify that the anonymous user password is the same in both User Manager for Domains and Internet Service Manager. These are distinct logons and passwords, and unified logon works only if their values are the same.

To prevent anonymous users from logging on to your site, when FTP is running on the server it constantly looks for activity on control port 21—its preassigned number. If you want to offer the service, yet hide its availability, you can do so by changing the port assignment from 21 to any open number greater than 1023. Alternatively, or additionally, you can disable anonymous access by unchecking the Allow Anonymous Access check box in the Authentication Methods dialog box for each site.

FTP usage statistics can be gathered from Performance Monitor using the Connection Attempts and Logon Attempts counters. The former will report when a host attempts to connect to a target anonymously, whereas the latter will indicate those times a connection other than anonymous was attempted.

WHAT IS IMPORTANT TO KNOW

The following bullets summarize the chapter and accentuate the key concepts to memorize for the exam:

- ◆ Content Analyzer's WebMaps can be used to administer Web site content to help you keep your Web site up to date and functioning correctly. You use the Link Info window, searches, and properties to help you manage your site's content.

- ◆ The three main parameters that specify how TCP/IP is configured are:

  - • The IP address (the network address and host address of the computer)

  - • The subnet mask (specifies what portion of the IP address specifies the network address and what portion of the address specifies the host address)

  - • The default gateway (most commonly, the address of the router).

- ◆ Using a DHCP server can greatly reduce TCP/IP configuration problems.

- ◆ Scopes are ranges of available addresses on a DHCP server. The most important part of the configuration is to make sure you don't have duplicate addresses in the different scopes.

- ◆ Most Index Server troubleshooting and correction is implemented automatically without administrator interaction.

- ◆ If Index Server is not running and a query comes in, Index Server will automatically start. Therefore, as an administrator, the starting of Index Server is not something you should ever need to manually do.

- ◆ As an administrator, the stopping of Index Server is something you should never need to do, either, but can do from the Services utility.

- ◆ One of the most common problems with using Index Server is that of running out of disk space. If the drive fills, indexing is paused, and the only method of knowing this is by a message written to the event log. The event log should be monitored routinely by an administrator for this and similar occurrences.

Think of this as your personal study diary. Your documentation of how you beat this exam.

The following section of Objective Review Notes is provided so you can personalize this book to maximum effect. This is your workbook, study sheet, notes section, whatever you want to call it. YOU will ultimately decide exactly what information you'll need, but there's no reason this information should be written down somewhere else. As the author has learned from his teaching experiences, there's absolutely no substitute for taking copious notes and using them throughout the study process.

There's a separate section—two to a page—for each subobjective covered in the book. Each subobjective section falls under the main exam objective category, just as you'd expect to find it. It is strongly suggested that you review each subobjective and immediately make note of your knowledge level; then return to the Objective Review Notes section repeatedly and document your progress. Your ultimate goal should be to be able to review this section alone and know if you are ready for the exam.

OBJECTIVE REVIEW NOTES

Suggested use:

1. Read the objective. Refer to the part of the book where it's covered. Then ask yourself the following questions:

   - Do you already know this material? Then check "Got it" and make a note of the date.

   - Do you need some brushing up on the objective area? Check "Review it" and make a note of the date. While you're at it, write down the page numbers you just checked, because you'll need to return to that section.

   - Is this material something you're largely unfamiliar with? Check the "Help!" box and write down the date. Now you can get to work.

2. You get the idea. Keep working through the material in this book and in the other study material you probably have. The better you understand the material, the quicker you can update and upgrade each objective notes section from "Help!" to "Review it" to "Got it."

3. Cross reference the materials YOU are using. Most people who take certification exams use more than one resource at a time. Write down the page numbers of where this material is covered in other books you're using, or which software program and file this material is covered on, or which video tape (and counter number) it's on, or whatever you need that works for you.

Planning

▶ Objective: Choose a security strategy for various situations.

☐ **Got it**　　☐ **Review it**　　☐ **Help!**
　*Date:*_____　*Date:*_____　*Date:*_____

Notes:

_____
_____
_____
_____
_____

Fast Track cross reference, see pages:

_____
_____

Other resources cross reference, see pages:

_____
_____
_____

▶ Objective: Choose an implementation stragegy for an Internet site or an intranet site for standalone servers, single-domain environments, and multiple-domain environments.

☐ **Got it**　　☐ **Review it**　　☐ **Help!**
　*Date:*_____　*Date:*_____　*Date:*_____

Notes:

_____
_____
_____
_____
_____

Fast Track cross reference, see pages:

_____
_____

Other resources cross reference, see pages:

_____
_____
_____

► Objective: Choose the appropriate technology to resolve specified problems.

☐ Got it	☐ Review it	☐ Help!
Date:	*Date:*	*Date:*

Notes:
_____
_____
_____
_____

Fast Track cross reference, see pages:
_____
_____

Other resources cross reference, see pages:
_____

Installation and Configuration

► Objective: Install IIS.

☐ Got it	☐ Review it	☐ Help!
Date:	*Date:*	*Date:*

Notes:
_____
_____
_____
_____

Fast Track cross reference, see pages:
_____
_____

Other resources cross reference, see pages:
_____

► Objective: Configure IIS to support the FTP Service.

☐ Got it	☐ Review it	☐ Help!
Date:	*Date:*	*Date:*

Notes:
_____
_____
_____
_____

Fast Track cross reference, see pages:

Other resources cross reference, see pages:

► Objective: Configure IIS to support the WWW Service.

☐ Got it   ☐ Review it   ☐ Help!
   Date:_____   Date:_____   Date:_____

Notes:

Fast Track cross reference, see pages:

Other resources cross reference, see pages:

►

Objective: Configure and save consoles by using Microsoft
Management Console.

☐ Got it   ☐ Review it   ☐ Help!
   Date:_____   Date:_____   Date:_____

Notes:

Fast Track cross reference, see pages:

Other resources cross reference, see pages:

▶Objective: Verify server settings by accessing the metabase.

☐ **Got it** ☐ **Review it** ☐ **Help!**
*Date:*_____ *Date:*_____ *Date:*_____

Notes:
_____
_____
_____
_____

Fast Track cross reference, see pages:
_____
_____

Other resources cross reference, see pages:
_____
_____

▶Objective: Choose the appropriate administration method.

☐ **Got it** ☐ **Review it** ☐ **Help!**
*Date:*_____ *Date:*_____ *Date:*_____

Notes:
_____
_____
_____
_____

Fast Track cross reference, see pages:
_____
_____

Other resources cross reference, see pages:
_____
_____

▶Objective: Install and configure Certificate Server.

☐ **Got it** ☐ **Review it** ☐ **Help!**
*Date:*_____ *Date:*_____ *Date:*_____

Notes:
_____
_____
_____
_____

OBJECTIVE REVIEW NOTES

Fast Track cross reference, see pages:

_____

_____

Other resources cross reference, see pages:

_____

_____

► Objective: Install and configure Microsoft SMTP Service.

☐ **Got it**   ☐ **Review it**   ☐ **Help!**
  *Date:*_____   *Date:*_____   *Date:*_____

Notes:

_____

_____

_____

_____

Fast Track cross reference, see pages:

_____

_____

Other resources cross reference, see pages:

_____

_____

► Objective: Install and configure Microsoft NNTP Service.

☐ **Got it**   ☐ **Review it**   ☐ **Help!**
  *Date:*_____   *Date:*_____   *Date:*_____

Notes:

_____

_____

_____

_____

Fast Track cross reference, see pages:

_____

_____

Other resources cross reference, see pages:

_____

_____

_____

OBJECTIVE REVIEW NOTES

►Objective: Customize the installation of Microsoft Site Server Express Analysis Content Analyzer.

☐ **Got it** ☐ **Review it** ☐ **Help!**
   *Date:*_____   *Date:*_____   *Date:*_____

Notes:
_____
_____
_____
_____

Fast Track cross reference, see pages:
_____
_____

Other resources cross reference, see pages:
_____
_____
_____
_____

►Objective: Customize the installation of Site Server Express Analysis Report Writer and Usage Import.

☐ **Got it** ☐ **Review it** ☐ **Help!**
   *Date:*_____   *Date:*_____   *Date:*_____

Notes:
_____
_____
_____
_____

Fast Track cross reference, see pages:
_____
_____

Other resources cross reference, see pages:
_____
_____
_____

OBJECTIVE REVIEW NOTES

Configuring and Managing Resource Access

► Objective: Create and share directories with appropriate permissions.

☐ Got it	☐ Review it	☐ Help!
Date:____	Date:_____	Date:____

Notes:

_____
_____
_____
_____

Fast Track cross reference, see pages:

_____
_____

Other resources cross reference, see pages:

_____
_____
_____

► Objective: Create and share local and remote virtual directories with appropriate permissions.

☐ Got it	☐ Review it	☐ Help!
Date:____	Date:_____	Date:____

Notes:

_____
_____
_____
_____

Fast Track cross reference, see pages:

_____
_____

Other resources cross reference, see pages:

_____
_____
_____

OBJECTIVE REVIEW NOTES

► Objective: Create and share virtual servers with appropriate permissions.

☐ **Got it** / ☐ **Review it** / ☐ **Help!**
*Date:*_____ *Date:*_____ *Date:*_____

Notes:
_____
_____
_____
_____

Fast Track cross reference, see pages:
_____
_____
_____

Other resources cross reference, see pages:
_____
_____

► Objective: Write scripts to manage the FTP service or the WWW service.

☐ **Got it** / ☐ **Review it** / ☐ **Help!**
*Date:*_____ *Date:*_____ *Date:*_____

Notes:
_____
_____
_____
_____

Fast Track cross reference, see pages:
_____
_____
_____

Other resources cross reference, see pages:
_____
_____

► Objective: Configure Microsoft NNTP Service to host a newsgroup.

☐ **Got it** / ☐ **Review it** / ☐ **Help!**
*Date:*_____ *Date:*_____ *Date:*_____

Notes:
_____
_____

Fast Track cross reference, see pages:

_____

_____

Other resources cross reference, see pages:

_____

_____

►Objective: Manage a Web site by using Content Analyzer.

☐ Got it	☐ Review it	☐ Help!
Date:____	Date:_____	Date:_____

Notes:

_____

_____

_____

_____

Fast Track cross reference, see pages:

_____

_____

Other resources cross reference, see pages:

_____

_____

_____

►Objective: Configure Microsoft SMTP Service to host personal mailboxes.

☐ Got it	☐ Review it	☐ Help!
Date:____	Date:_____	Date:_____

Notes:

_____

_____

_____

_____

Fast Track cross reference, see pages:

_____

_____

Other resources cross reference, see pages:

_____

_____

_____

OBJECTIVE REVIEW NOTES

OBJECTIVE REVIEW NOTES

► Objective: Configure Index Server to index a Web site.

☐ Got it	☐ Review it	☐ Help!
Date:____	Date:_____	Date:_____

Notes:
_____
_____
_____
_____

Fast Track cross reference, see pages:
_____
_____

Other resources cross reference, see pages:
_____
_____

Objective: Manage MIME types.

☐ Got it	☐ Review it	☐ Help!
Date:____	Date:_____	Date:_____

► Notes:
_____
_____
_____
_____

Fast Track cross reference, see pages:
_____
_____

Other resources cross reference, see pages:
_____
_____

Objective: Configure Certificate Server to issue certificates.

☐ Got it	☐ Review it	☐ Help!
Date:____	Date:_____	Date:_____

Notes:
_____
_____
_____
_____

Fast Track cross reference, see pages:

_____
_____

Other resources cross reference, see pages:

_____
_____
_____

►**Objective: Manage the FTP Service.**

| ☐ **Got it** | ☐ **Review it** | ☐ **Help!** |
| *Date:_____* | *Date:_____* | *Date:_____* |

Notes:

_____
_____
_____
_____

Fast Track cross reference, see pages:

_____
_____

Other resources cross reference, see pages:

_____
_____

►**Objective: Manage the WWW Service.**

| ☐ **Got it** | ☐ **Review it** | ☐ **Help!** |
| *Date:_____* | *Date:_____* | *Date:_____* |

Notes:

_____
_____
_____
_____

Fast Track cross reference, see pages:

_____
_____

Other resources cross reference, see pages:

_____
_____
_____

OBJECTIVE REVIEW NOTES

Integration and Interoperability

►Objective: Configure IIS to connect to a database.

☐ **Got it**   ☐ **Review it**   ☐ **Help!**
Date: *Date:*   *Date:*

Notes:
_____
_____
_____
_____
_____
_____

Fast Track cross reference, see pages:
_____
_____

Other resources cross reference, see pages:
_____
_____
_____
_____

►Objective: Configure IIS to integrate with Index Server.

☐ **Got it**   ☐ **Review it**   ☐ **Help!**
Date: *Date:*   *Date:*

Notes:
_____
_____
_____
_____

Fast Track cross reference, see pages:
_____
_____

Other resources cross reference, see pages:
_____
_____
_____

OBJECTIVE REVIEW NOTES

Running Applications

► Objective: Configure IIS to support server-side scripting.

☐ Got it	☐ Review it	☐ Help!
Date:____	Date:_____	Date:____

Notes:

_____

_____

_____

_____

_____

Fast Track cross reference, see pages:

_____

_____

Other resources cross reference, see pages:

_____

_____

_____

► Objective: Configure IIS to run ISAPI applications.

☐ Got it	☐ Review it	☐ Help!
Date:____	Date:_____	Date:____

Notes:

_____

_____

_____

Fast Track cross reference, see pages:

_____

_____

Other resources cross reference, see pages:

_____

_____

_____

OBJECTIVE REVIEW NOTES

▶Objective: Configure IIS to support ADO associated with the WWW Service.

☐ Got it   ☐ Review it   ☐ Help!
   Date:_____   Date:_____   Date:_____

Notes:

_____

_____

_____

_____

_____

Fast Track cross reference, see pages:

_____

_____

Other resources cross reference, see pages:

_____

_____

_____

_____

Monitoring and Optimization

▶Objective: Maintain a log for fine-tuning and auditing purposes.

☐ Got it   ☐ Review it   ☐ Help!
   Date:_____   Date:_____   Date:_____

Notes:

_____

_____

_____

_____

Fast Track cross reference, see pages:

_____

_____

Other resources cross reference, see pages:

_____

_____

► Objective: Monitor performance of various functions by using Performance Monitor.

☐ **Got it**   ☐ **Review it**   ☐ **Help!**
   Date: *Date:*   *Date:*

Notes:

_____
_____
_____
_____
_____

Fast Track cross reference, see pages:

_____
_____

Other resources cross reference, see pages:

_____
_____
_____
_____

► Objective: Analyze performance.

☐ **Got it**   ☐ **Review it**   ☐ **Help!**
   Date: *Date:*   *Date:*

Notes:

_____
_____
_____
_____
_____

Fast Track cross reference, see pages:

_____
_____

Other resources cross reference, see pages:

_____
_____
_____

OBJECTIVE REVIEW NOTES

►Objective: Optimize performance of IIS.

☐ Got it	☐ Review it	☐ Help!
*Date:*___	*Date:*_____	*Date:*_____

Notes:
_____
_____
_____
_____
_____
_____

Fast Track cross reference, see pages:
_____
_____

Other resources cross reference, see pages:
_____
_____
_____
_____

►Objective: Optimize performance of Index Server.

☐ Got it	☐ Review it	☐ Help!
*Date:*___	*Date:*_____	*Date:*_____

Notes:
_____
_____
_____
_____
_____
_____

Fast Track cross reference, see pages:
_____
_____

Other resources cross reference, see pages:
_____
_____
_____

OBJECTIVE REVIEW NOTES

► Objective: Optimize performance of Microsoft SMTP Service.

☐ Got it	☐ Review it	☐ Help!
Date:_____	Date:_____	Date:_____

Notes:

_____
_____
_____
_____
_____
_____

Fast Track cross reference, see pages:

_____
_____

Other resources cross reference, see pages:

_____
_____
_____
_____

► Objective: Optimize performance of Microsoft NNTP Service.

☐ Got it	☐ Review it	☐ Help!
Date:_____	Date:_____	Date:_____

Notes:

_____
_____
_____
_____
_____
_____

Fast Track cross reference, see pages:

_____
_____

Other resources cross reference, see pages:

_____
_____
_____

OBJECTIVE REVIEW NOTES

OBJECTIVE REVIEW NOTES

► Objective: Interpret performance data.

☐ **Got it**   ☐ **Review it**   ☐ **Help!**
    Date:_____   *Date:_____*   *Date:_____*

Notes:
_____
_____
_____
_____
_____

Fast Track cross reference, see pages:
_____
_____

Other resources cross reference, see pages:
_____
_____
_____
_____

► Objective: Optimize a Web site by using Content Analyzer.

☐ **Got it**   ☐ **Review it**   ☐ **Help!**
    Date:_____   *Date:_____*   *Date:_____*

Notes:
_____
_____
_____
_____

Fast Track cross reference, see pages:
_____
_____

Other resources cross reference, see pages:
_____
_____
_____
_____

Troubleshooting

Objective: Resolve IIS configuration problems.

☐ **Got it**
Date:_____

☐ **Review it**
Date:_____

☐ **Help!**
Date:_____

Notes:

_____

_____

_____

_____

_____

_____

Fast Track cross reference, see pages:

_____

_____

Other resources cross reference, see pages:

_____

_____

_____

_____

Objective: Resolve security problems.

☐ **Got it**
Date:_____

☐ **Review it**
Date:_____

☐ **Help!**
Date:_____

Notes:

_____

_____

_____

_____

Fast Track cross reference, see pages:

_____

_____

Other resources cross reference, see pages:

_____

_____

_____

_____

_____

▶Objective: Resolve resource access problems.

☐ **Got it**
Date:_____

☐ **Review it**
Date:_____

☐ **Help!**
Date:_____

Notes:
_____
_____
_____
_____
_____

Fast Track cross reference, see pages:
_____

Other resources cross reference, see pages:
_____
_____
_____

▶Objective: Resolve Index Server query problems.

☐ **Got it**
Date:_____

☐ **Review it**
Date:_____

☐ **Help!**
Date:_____

Notes:
_____
_____
_____
_____
_____

Fast Track cross reference, see pages:
_____

Other resources cross reference, see pages:
_____
_____
_____

OBJECTIVE REVIEW NOTES

Objective: Resolve setup issues when installing IIS on a Windows NT Server 4.0 computer.

☐ **Got it**   ☐ **Review it**   ☐ **Help!**
Date:_____   Date:_____   Date:_____

Notes:

_____

_____

_____

_____

_____

Fast Track cross reference, see pages:

_____

_____

Other resources cross reference, see pages:

_____

_____

_____

Objective: Use a WebMap to find and repair broken links, hyperlink texts, headings, and titles.

☐ **Got it**   ☐ **Review it**   ☐ **Help!**
Date:_____   Date:_____   Date:_____

Notes:

_____

_____

_____

_____

_____

Fast Track cross reference, see pages:

_____

_____

Other resources cross reference, see pages:

_____

_____

_____

_____

OBJECTIVE REVIEW NOTES

▶Objective: Resolve WWW service problems.

☐ Got it   ☐ Review it   ☐ Help!
   Date: *Date:*   *Date:*

Notes:

_____
_____
_____
_____
_____
_____

Fast Track cross reference, see pages:

_____
_____

Other resources cross reference, see pages:

_____
_____
_____
_____

▶Objective: Resolve FTP service problems.

☐ Got it   ☐ Review it   ☐ Help!
   Date: *Date:*   *Date:*

Notes:

_____
_____
_____
_____
_____
_____

Fast Track cross reference, see pages:

_____
_____

Other resources cross reference, see pages:

_____
_____
_____
_____

INSIDE EXAM 70-087

Part II of this book is designed to round out your exam preparation by providing you with chapters that do the following:

▶ "Fast Facts Review" is a digest of all "What Is Important to Know" sections from all Part I chapters. Use this chapter to review just before you take the exam: It's all here, in an easily reviewable format.

▶ "Insider's Spin on Exam 70-087" grounds you in the particulars for preparing mentally for this examination and for Microsoft testing in general.

▶ "Sample Test Questions" provides a full-length practice exam that tests you on the actual material covered in Part I. If you mastered the material there, you should be able to pass with flying colors here.

▶ "Hotlist of Exam-Critical Concepts" is your resource for cross-checking your tech terms. Although you're probably up to speed on most of this material already, double-check yourself anytime you run across an item you're not 100% certain about; it could make a difference at exam time.

▶ "Did You Know?" is the last-day-of-class bonus chapter: A brief touching-upon of peripheral information designed to be helpful and of interest to anyone using this technology to the point that they want to be certified in its mastery.

OBJECTIVES

The exam is divided into seven objective categories:

▶ **Planning**

▶ **Installation and Configuration**

▶ **Configuring and Managing Resources**

▶ **Integration and Interoperability**

▶ **Running Applications**

▶ **Monitoring and Optimization**

▶ **Troubleshooting**

CHAPTER **8**

Fast Facts Review

WHAT TO STUDY

A review of the key topics discussed in the preceding seven chapters follows. After you are certain that you understand the principles given in those seven chapters, study these key points on the day of the exam prior to writing it.

Planning

As with previous IIS exams, the WWW service and FTP service are the core areas the exam focuses on. IIS can be installed on a standalone machine, or in almost any other configuration. It can be installed on a workstation or server, but a workstation should only be used as a test environment, as it is not suitable for most purposes.

Remember that **IIS automatically creates a user account upon installation with the username of IUSR_*computername*.** This is the account used for anonymous access and granted Log on Locally user rights by default. The account is necessary for anonymous logon access to your Web site, and permissions applied to it control the permissions for the anonymous user. You can even go so far as to disable anonymous access if security is a concern.

For the WWW service, **available authentication methods** are:

- **Allow Anonymous Access**. Enables clients to connect to your Web site without requiring a username or password by using the default account of IUSR_*computername*.

- **Basic Authentication**. This method is used if you do not specify anonymous access and you want a client connecting to your Web site to enter a valid Windows NT username and password to log on. This sends a password in clear text format with the passwords being transmitted in an unencrypted format.

- **Windows NT Challenge/Response**. This setting is used if you want the Windows NT Challenge/Response feature to authenticate the client attempting to connect to your Web site. The **only Web browsers that support this feature include Internet Explorer 2.0 and later**. During the challenge/response procedure, cryptographic information is exchanged between the client and server to authenticate the user.

For the FTP service, available authentication methods include the ability to specify that anonymous connections are allowed, only anonymous connections are allowed, or the administrator can configure user and group accounts. Although it makes perfect sense, on the exam know that you cannot specify that only anonymous connections are allowed until you have first allowed anonymous connections.

Know the basics of TCP/IP (including what WINS and DNS are) and **IP values**, namely the number of hosts available per IP address class as recapped in the table below:

Class	Address	Number of Hosts Available	Default Subnet Mask
A	01-126	16,777,214	255.0.0.0
B	128-191	65,534	255.255.0.0
C	192-223	254	255.255.255.0

The WINS service is used for dynamic resolution of NetBIOS names to IP addresses, whereas **DNS is used for resolution of host names to IP addresses**. The counterparts of each for small installations are the LMHOSTS and HOSTS files, respectively.

Secure Sockets Layer—or SSL—enables you to **protect communications over a network** whether that network is an intranet or the Internet. It does so by establishing a private (and encrypted) communication link between the user and the server. SSL can be used not only to authenticate specific users, but also the anonymous user. If SSL is enabled and a user attempts anonymous access, the Web server will look for a valid certificate on the client and reject those lacking such. To use SSL, you must obtain a digital certificate from an authentication authority and use Key Manager to generate keys. SSL URLs begin with `https://` instead of `http://`. The default configuration of SSL does not look for client-side certificates.

Memorize the table of subnets and the number of hosts that using each makes available on a C-level network:

Last digits of Subnet Address	Number of Addresses in Range
192	64
224	32
240	16
248	8
252	4
254	2
255	1 (not used)

Installation and Configuration

To install IIS 4.0, you must first remove any previous versions of IIS (IIS 3.0, or 2.0 that came with NT 4.0). During the installation, you are prompted which services you want to install.

If you choose not to install a service at this time, you can restart the installation routine at any time and choose only the additional services you want to add. IIS 4.0 Hardware Requirements for an Intel System are:

Hardware Device	Requirements
CPU	Minimum of a 33MHZ (90 MHZ recommended) 486 DX processor. For better performance, you need a Pentium 133 or higher processor.
Hard disk space	Minimum of 30MB, but it is recommended you have **at least 120MB**. This does not include storage needed for files you plan to distribute via IIS.
Memory	**Minimum of 32MB**. For a Web site on which you will store multimedia files or expect a great deal of traffic, 48MB is the recommended minimum.
Monitor	**Super VGA monitor** with 800×600 resolution.

TCP Port settings are used by clients to connect to your FTP or WWW site. Memorize default port settings:

Service	Port
FTP	**21**
SMTP	**25**
WWW	**80**
NNTP	**119**
SSL	**443**
NNTP with SSL	**563**

You can change the settings to unique TCP port numbers, but you must announce this setting to all clients who want to access your server.

An FTP **directory listing style** is the way in which your server will display a directory listing. The two choices are DOS (such as C:\folder\ subfolder), or UNIX format (such as C:/directory/subdirectory/). **Use UNIX format for the greatest compatibility on the Internet**.

Limiting bandwidth is known as *throttling bandwidth*, and limits only the bandwidth used by the Web service. IIS 4.0 provides support for HTTP 1.1 Host Headers in order to allow multiple host names to be associated with one IP address. With this feature, a separate IP address is not needed for every virtual server you support. Microsoft Internet Explorer 3.0 and later and Netscape Navigator 2.0 and later support this feature, but many other browsers do not.

IIS 4.0's **Keep-Alive** feature **enables clients to maintain open connections**. This way, a client does not need to re-establish connections for each request. By enabling Keep-Alives, you decrease the amount of time a client waits to connect to another document or application on your site. But you also increase the amount of resources devoted to this client.

Configuring and Managing Resource Access

The Microsoft Management Console is the primary utility used for most tasks. Accessed by choosing Internet Service Manager from the Programs menu, it is used for almost everything, including creating and sharing new directories, virtual directories, or servers. If there is only one thing you need to learn for the exam, it is everything you possibly can about MMC.

Access permissions for directories include:

- Allow Read Access
- Allow Script Access
- Allow Execute Access
- Allow Write Access
- Allow Directory Browsing

The five rights that you can select for IIS access work in conjunction with all other rights. Like share rights, the **IIS rights are *in addition to* NTFS rights**, and of greatest value when you are using anonymous access. Allowing Read access lets a user view a file if her NTFS permissions also allow such. Taking away Read, however, prevents the user from viewing the file regardless of what NTFS may do.

The names of the rights are pretty self-explanatory as to what they offer. The only caveats to note are that Read and Script access are assigned by default, and Execute is a superset of Script access.

With virtual directories (which must exist on servers all within the same NT domain) you can get around issues such as disk space, determining where best to store files, and so on. There are two downfalls to using virtual directories:

- A slight decrease in performance as files must be retrieved from the LAN, rather than being centralized.

- Virtual directories do not show up in WWW listings, and must be accessed through explicit links within HTML files.

You should also **have a scripts directory under every virtual home directory to handle the executables there**.

The Internet Service Manager (HTML) can let you manage the FTP and WWW service remotely (WWW must first be running in order to use this). Remotely, you can do almost everything you can locally with the exception of making MIME Registry changes or stopping and starting services (if you stopped WWW, you would be disconnected).

MIME is used to define the type of file sent to the browser based on the extension. If your server is supplying files in multiple formats, it must have a MIME mapping for each file type or browsers will most likely be unable to retrieve the file. Mappings can be added or changed with REGEDIT or REGEDT32.

Integration and Interoperability

Databases such as Oracle or Microsoft SQL (Structured Query Language) Server can be used with IIS to supply the information to fulfill a query, update information, and add new data through the Web almost as easily as if a user were sitting on a local area network.

Open Database Connectivity (ODBC) is an Application Programming Interface (API) that provides a simple way to connect to an existing database (whether that database by SQL or any ODBC-compliant database). It was designed by Microsoft to provide a standard for connecting to databases. **ODBC can be used to connect to SQL servers**, but it was initially designed to provide connectivity to a broad range of databases. Authentication can be done by Windows NT or SQL. If SQL is chosen, it uses standard logon security and a SQL Server user ID and password must be given for all connections. If you choose to use Windows NT authentication, the Windows NT user account is associated with a SQL Server user account, and integrated security is used to establish the connection regardless of the current security mode at the server (similar to how IUSR_*computername* is used for anonymous access to a site).

The **greatest advantage that ODBC offers is that it defines a clear distinction between the application and the database**, and thus does not require any specific programming. To use it, you create a query and template for how the output is to look.

There are four major components to IIS's implementation of ODBC, and they are:

- .HTM—the file containing the hyperlink for a query. The request comes from the browser and merely specifies the URL for the .IDC (Internet Database Connector) file on IIS.

- .HTX—a file of HTML extensions containing the template document with placeholders for the result. Database fields that it receives are known as containers, and are identified by field names surrounded by percents (%) and braces (<>). Thus the `employeeno` field that comes from the SQL database is known as `<%employeeno%>` here. All processing is done in loops that start with `<%begindetail%>` and end with `<%enddetail%>`. Logic can be included with `<%if...%>` and `<%endif%>`, as well as `<%else%>` statements.

- .IDC—the file containing the data source file information and SQL statement. Four required parameters are `Datasource`, `Username`, `Template`, and `SQLStatement`. The `SQLStatement` is the list of commands you want to execute. Parameter values can be used if they are enclosed in percents (%), and if multiple lines are required, a plus sign (+) must be the first character on each line.

- Httpodbc.dll—the dynamic link library included with the server.

Index Server differs from the ODBC discussion in the files used to hold the queries. Rather than using the .IDC file, Index Server uses an .IDQ (Internet Data Query) file. The .IDQ file should always be placed in the Scripts directory, and it requires Execute or Script permission to properly function.

There are two sections to the file and it begins with a tag of [Query] (the first section) and followed by the [Names] section. The Names section is purely optional, and not used most of the time. If it is used, it defines nonstandard column names that are referred to in a query. The Query section of the file is all that is required, and it can contain parameters, variables, and conditional expressions.

Restrictions are that lines must start with the variable you are trying to set, and only one variable can be set per line. Additionally, percents (%) are used to identify the variables and references.

As with most script files, a pound sign (#) can be used to specify a comment. At whatever point the # sign is in the line, the rest of the line will be ignored. The conditional expressions that can be used with .IDQ files are the following:

- **CONTAINS—is true if any part of the first value is found in the second value**
- **EQ—equal to**
- **GE—greater than or equal to**
- **GT—greater than**
- **ISEMPTY—is true if the value is null**
- **LE—less than or equal to**
- **LT—less than**
- **NE—not equal to**

Running Applications

ISAPI—Internet Server API (Application Programming Interface)—can be used to write applications that Web users can activate by filling out an HTML form or clicking a link in an HTML page on your Web server. The user-supplied information can then be responded to and the results returned in an HTML page or posted to a database.

ISAPI was a Microsoft **improvement over** popular **CGI (Common Gateway Interface)** scripting, and offers much better performance over CGI because applications are loaded into memory at server runtime. This means that they require less overhead and each request does not start a separate process. Additionally, ISAPI applications are created as DLLs on the server, and allow preprocessing of requests and post-processing of responses, permitting site-specific handling of HTTP requests and responses.

ISAPI filters can be used for applications such as customized authentication, access, or logging. You can create complex sites by combining ISAPI filters and applications.

ISAPI works with OLE connectivity and the Internet Database Connector. This allows ISAPI to be implemented as a DLL (in essence, an executable) or as a filter (translating another executable's output). If ISAPI is used as a filter, it is not called by the browser' accessing an URL, but rather summoned by the server in response to an event (which could easily be an URL request). Common uses of ISAPI filters include:

- Tracking URL usage statistics

- Performing authentication

- Adding entries to log files

- Compression

You don't need to be an ISAPI programmer to pass the exam, but there are several things you need to know:

- ISAPI applications effectively extend server applications to the desktop

- ISAPI is similar to CGI but offers better performance; CGI needs a new process for every execution

- Although created by Microsoft, ISAPI is an open specification that third-parties can write to

- ISAPI filters can do pre- or post-processing

- Execute, but not necessarily read permission is required for CGI or ISAPI script execution

Monitoring and Optimization

The Active Log Format drop-down list lets you select the type of log format you want to create. The following are the supported log file formats:

- **Microsoft IIS Log Format**. This is a fixed ASCII format that records basic logging items, including username, request date, request time, client IP address, number of bytes received, HTTP status code, and other items. This is a comma-delimited log file, making it easier to parse than other ASCII formats.

- **NCSA Common Log File Format**. This is a fixed ASCII format endorsed by the National Center for Supercomputing Applications (NCSA). The data it logs includes remote hostname, username, HTTP status code, request type, and the number of bytes received by the server. Spaces separate different items logged.

- **ODBC Logging**. This is a fixed format that **is logged to a database**. This log includes client IP address, username, request date, request time, HTTP status code, bytes received, bytes sent, action carried out, and the target. When you choose this option, you must specify the database for the file to be logged to. In addition, you must set up the database to receive that log data.

- **W3C Extended Log File Format**. This **is a customizable ASCII format** endorsed by the World Wide Web Consortium (W3C). This is the default setting. You can set this log format to record a number of different settings such as request date, request time, client IP address, server IP address, server port, HTTP status code, and more (see Table 8.1). Data is separated by spaces in this format.

TABLE 8.1

W3C EXTENDED LOG FILE FORMAT LOGGING OPTIONS

Option	Description
Date	Date the activity occurred.
Time	Time activity occurred.
Client IP Address	IP address of the client attaching to your server.
User Name	Username who accessed your server.
Service Name	Client computer's Internet service.
Server Name	Server name where the log entry was created.
Server IP	Server IP address where the log entry was created.
Server Port	Port number to which the client is connected.
Method	Action the client was performing.
URI Stem	Logs the resource the client was accessing on your server, such as an HTML page, CGI program, and so on.
URI Query	Logs the search string the client was trying to match.
HTTP Status	Status (in HTTP terms) of the client action.
Win32 Status	Status (in Windows NT terms) of the client action.
Bytes Sent	Number of bytes sent by the server.
Bytes Received	Number of bytes received by the server.
Time Taken	Amount of time to execute the action requested by the client.
User Agent	Browser used by the client.
Cookie	Content of any cookies sent or received by the server.
Protocol Version	The version of the protocol in use by the client.
Referrer	URL of the site from where the user clicked on to get to your site.

In the New Log Time Period section of the site's configuration, you set when you want IIS to create a new log file for the selected Web site. The default is Daily, but you can select Weekly, Monthly, Unlimited File Size, or When File Size Reaches. If you select the last option, you need to set a maximum file size the log file can reach before a new file is created. The default is 19MB. The default directory in which you store log files is %WinDir\System32\LogFiles.

The **Report Writer and Usage Import Database help you analyze and create reports based on logs** created by IIS. The main difference between Report Writer and Usage Import is that Report Writer creates analysis reports based on the log file data. Usage Import, on the other hand, reads the log files and places the data into a relational database.

Performance Monitor is used when you want to see trends and patterns of your site's usage. When you install IIS, new objects relating to Web and FTP services are added to Performance Monitor along with specific counters for those services. Objects are individual occurrences of a system resource, such as Web Service, FTP Service, Active Server Pages, Browser, and other items. Counters, on the other hand, are statistics relating to the objects, such as Debugging Requests, Memory Allocated, and Request Wait Time (all of which relate to the Active Server Pages object).

Bottlenecks occur when one (or several) hardware resource is being used too much, usually resulting in the draining of another hardware resource. The result is a performance reduction over the entire network. A bottleneck may occur as a result of insufficient server memory or because of too little bandwidth available to the connected users.

Start **looking for bottlenecks by running Performance Monitor to create a baseline** of activities for your site. You also can use Event Viewer to records events and audits situations on your computer that may require your attention. Another useful tool to use to locate bottlenecks is the Task Manager. Task Manager shows you all the ongoing tasks and threads on your computer.

For medium to very busy sites, you can expect IIS to saturate a 10MB Ethernet network adapter. This will certainly cause bottlenecks to occur that are network-related. To check for network saturation, check for CPU % Utilization on both the client and server. To prevent the server from becoming network bound, try one of the following solutions:

♦ Use multiple 10MB Ethernet cards, or

♦ Install a 100MB Ethernet or FDDI network card.

♦ Alternatively, consider taking advantage of a higher speed BUS architecture. For example, upgrading from an ISA card to PCI.

CPU bottlenecks can be identified by measuring the amount of the server CPU that is being utilized. If the CPU % Processor Time value is high, try the following remedies:

- **Upgrade the CPU to a faster one.**

- Add additional CPUs to your server.

- Move any CPU-intensive applications (such as database applications) you run on the Web server to another computer.

- Add more computers on which you replicate your site and then distribute traffic across them.

To optimize the performance of Index Server, you should start by looking at the configuration of the computer on which it resides. The following are the factors that you need to measure to set this configuration:

- Number of documents in the corpus, which is the collection of documents and HTML pages indexed by Index Server.

- Corpus size

- Rate of search requests

- Kind of queries

You'll find that the amount of memory you have installed will greatly affect the performance of Index Server. For sites that have fewer than 100,000 documents stored in the corpus, a minimum of 32MB is required and recommended. However, if you have over 100,000 up to 250,000 documents, the recommended amount of memory jumps to 64–128MB,whereas the minimum required still is 32MB. For sites with 250,000 to 500,000 documents, you need a minimum of 64MB of RAM, but **it is recommended that you have 128–256MB**. Finally, if you have over 500,000 documents, you must have at least 128MB of RAM installed, but 256MB is recommended.

Troubleshooting

Content Analyzer's WebMaps can be used to administer Web site content to help you keep your Web site up to date and functioning correctly. You use the Link Info window, searches, and properties to help you manage your site's content.

The three main parameters that specify how TCP/IP is configured are:

- The IP address (the network address and host address of the computer)

- The subnet mask (specifies what portion of the IP address specifies the network address and what portion of the address specifies the host address)

- The default gateway (most commonly, the address of the router)

Using a **DHCP server can greatly reduce TCP/IP configuration problems**. Scopes are ranges of available addresses on a DHCP server. The most important part of the configuration is to make sure you don't have duplicate addresses in the different scopes.

Most Index Server troubleshooting and correction is implemented automatically without administrator interaction.

If Index Server is not running and a query comes in, Index Server will automatically start. Therefore, as an administrator, the starting of Index Server is not something you should ever need to manually do. As an administrator, the stopping of Index Server is something you should never need to do, either, but can do from the Services utility.

Running out of disk space is one of the most common problems with using Index Server. If the drive fills, indexing is paused, and the only method of knowing this is by a message written to the event log. The event log should be monitored routinely by an administrator for this and similar occurrences.

In the Insider's Spin, you get the author's word on exam details specific to 70-087, as well as information you possibly didn't know—but could definitely benefit from—about what's behind Microsoft's exam preparation methodology. This chapter is designed to deepen your understanding of the entire Microsoft exam process. Use it as an extra edge: inside info brought to you by someone who teaches this material for a living.

CHAPTER 9

Insider's Spin on Exam 70-087

At A Glance: Exam Information

Exam Number	70-087
Minutes	90*
Questions	60*
Passing Score	666*
Single Answer Questions:	Yes
Multiple Answer with Correct Number Given	Yes
Multiple Answer Without Correct Number Given	Minimal
Ranking Order	Yes
Choices of A–D	Yes
Choices of A–E	No
Objective Categories	7

NOTE

These exam criteria will no longer apply when this exam goes to an adaptive format.

Exam 70-087, Implementing and Supporting Microsoft Internet Information Server 4.0, or the IIS exam as it is more commonly referred to, is computer-administered and intended to measure your ability to implement and manage the product. There are 60 questions asked, and a candidate has 90 minutes to answer them with a passing score of at least 666 (roughly translating to passing with 40 right answers).

There are four types of multiple choice questions on the exam—single answer (always readily identified by a radio button), multiple answer with and without the correct number to choose given, ranking order questions, and the new "simulated" questions. On the latter, an MMC emulator appears and you are asked to perform a specific task. On average, almost 20% of the questions asked are this format.

Although Microsoft no longer releases specific exam information, at one time it was quoted that 85% of all who take a certification exam fail it. Common logic then indicates that only 15 out of every 100 people who think they know a product know it well enough to pass—a remarkably low number.

Quite often, administrators who *do* know a product very well and use it on a daily basis fail certification exams. Is it because they don't know the product as well as they think they do? Sometimes, but more often than not, it is because of other factors:

- They know the product from the real-world perspective, and not from Microsoft's perspective.

- They are basing their answers on the product as it currently exists, and not on when it was first released.

- They are not accustomed to so many questions in such a short time, or they are not accustomed to the electronic test engine.

- They don't use all the testing tools available to them.

The purpose of this chapter is to try to prepare you for the exam and help you overcome these four items. If you've been taking exams on a daily basis, and don't think you need this information, skim the chapter and go on—odds are that you will still uncover some tips that can help you. On the other hand, if you have not taken a lot of electronic exams, or have been having difficulty passing them by as wide a margin as you should, read this chapter carefully.

GET INTO MICROSOFT'S MINDSET

When taking the exams, remember that Microsoft is the party responsible for the authoring of the exam. Microsoft employees do not actually write the exams themselves, but instead experts in the field are hired on a contract basis for each exam to write questions. All questions, however, must adhere to certain standards and be approved by Microsoft before they make it into the actual exam. What that translates into is that Microsoft will never have anything in an exam that reflects negatively on them. They will also use the exams for promotional marketing as much as possible.

Therefore, in order to successfully answer questions, and pass the exams, you must put yourself into the Microsoft mindset and see questions from their standpoint. Take the following question for example:

1. Which network operating system is the easiest to administer in a small real-estate office?

A. NetWare 3.12

B. SCO UNIX

C. Windows NT 4.0

D. LAN Server

While you could look at the question and make a sincere argument for at least three of the answers, there is only one that will be correct on a Microsoft exam. Don't try to read too much between the lines, and don't think that you're going to put a comment at the end of the exam arguing your case why another choice would be better—if you answer anything other than C, you might as well write this one off as a missed question.

UNDERSTAND THE TIME FRAME OF THE EXAM

When you take an exam, find out when it was written. In almost all cases, an exam goes live within 3 months of the final release of the product it is based on. Prior to the release of the exam, it goes through a beta process where all of the questions that can be on the exam are written. It is then available for a short time (typically a week) during which scores on each question can be gathered. Questions that exam takers get right every time are weeded out as being too easy, and those that are too hard are weeded out as well.

When you take something like a major operating system (to remain nameless in this example) and create an exam for it, what you end up with is a time frame similar to the following:

1. Product goes into early beta.

2. A survey is taken (mostly of beta testers) to find out which components of the product they spend most time with and consider to be the most important. Their findings are used to generate the objectives and the weighting for each.

3. Product goes to final beta.

4. Contract writers are hired to write questions on the product using the findings from the survey.

5. Product goes live.

6. Exam is beta tested for one to two weeks, after which, results on each question are evaluated, and the final question pool is chosen.

7. Service pack for the product is released.

8. Exam goes live.

9. Another service pack to fix problems from the first service pack and add additional functionality is released.

10. Yet another service pack comes out.

11. Option Pack—incorporating service packs—is released.

12. You take the exam.

Now suppose the product happens to be NT Server 4, and you receive a question such as:

1. What is the maximum number of processors NT Server 4.0 can handle?

    A. 2

    B. 4

    C. 8

    D. 16

In the real world, the answer is D. When NT 4.0 first came out, however, the answer was B. Since the original exam questions were written to the final beta, the answer then was B, and is now B. Microsoft has maintained the stance that they will only test on core products, and not add-ons. Service Packs, Option Packs, and the like are considered something other than core product.

With this in mind, you must *always* answer every question as if you are addressing the product as it exists when you pull it from the box, and before you do anything else with it—because that is exactly what the exam is written to. You must get into this mindset and understand the time frame in which the exam was written, or you will fail exams consistently.

GET USED TO ANSWERING QUESTIONS QUICKLY

Every exam has a different number of questions asked, and most stick with the 90-minute time frame in which to do so. If you run out of time, every question you have not answered is graded as a wrong answer. Therefore:

- Always answer every single question, and never leave any unanswered. If you start running out of time, answer all the remaining questions with the same answer (C, D, etc.) then go back and start reading them. Using the law of averages, if you do run out of time, you should get 25% of the remaining ones correct.

- Time yourself carefully. A clock runs at the top right of each screen. Mark all questions that require lots of reading, or have exhibits and come back to them after you've answered all the shorter questions.

- Practice, practice, practice. Get accustomed to electronic questioning and answering questions in a short period of time. With as many exam simulators as there are available, there is no reason for anyone to not run through one or two before plunking down $100 for the real thing. Some of the simulators are not worth the code they're written in, and others are so close in style to the actual exam that they prepare you very well. If money is an issue, and it should be, look for demos and freebies on Web sites. For a great sample that is accessible over the Web, go to http://www.MeasureUp.com where you can try some sample exams online.

When you get into a situation where you do run out of time, spend as much time as you want to on the last question. You will never time out with a question in front of you, and will only be timed out when you click Next to go from that question to the next one.

BECOME ACQUAINTED WITH ALL THE RESOURCES AVAILABLE TO YOU

An enormous amount of common sense is important here, and much of that common sense only comes as you get more used to the testing procedure. To summarize a typical sequence of events:

1. You study for an exam for a considerable period of time.

2. You call Sylvan Prometric (1-800-755-EXAM) and register for the exam.

3. You drive to the testing site, sit in your car, and cram on those last-minute details that won't stick with the others.

4. You walk into the center, sign your name, show two forms of ID, and walk back to a computer.

5. Someone enters your ID in the computer and leaves. You're left with the computer, two pieces of plain paper, and two #2 pencils.

6. You click the button on the screen to begin the exam and the 90 minutes begin.

When you call Sylvan, be certain to ask how many questions are on the exam, so you know before you go in. There is very little information Sylvan is allowed to release (for example, they can't tell you the passing score) and this is one of the few pieces of information they can pass along.

The exam begins the minute you click the button to start it. Prior to that time, your 90 minutes haven't started. Once you walk into the testing center and sit down, you're free (within reason) to do whatever you want to. Why not dump everything from your brain (including those last-minute facts you just crammed in the parking lot) onto those two sheets of paper before starting the exam? The two sheets provide you with four sides—more than enough to scribble out everything you've remembered —and you can refer to them during the 90 minutes.

Once you click Start, the first question appears. There are a number of different types of questions that are asked, and Figure 9.1 shows but one. Because Microsoft does not readily make available (for obvious reasons) the ability to take screen shots of the exams, Figure 9.1 and all figures in this chapter, are from a third-party emulator closely resembling the real thing.

Look at the question briefly, but more importantly, look at the information on the screen. First, you have the ability to mark this question; doing so will allow you to see (at the end of the exam) any questions you thought were difficult and to jump back to them. Never mark a question and go to the next one without choosing some answer. Even if you don't read the question at all and are saving it for later, mark it and answer C. That way if you run out of time, you have a chance of getting it right.

In the right-hand corner, you see the question number that you are on. In the real exam, you also see the time remaining here. Beneath the question are the possible answers. The radio buttons to the left of each answer choice indicate that there can only be one possible correct answer.

While not always true, many times when there are four possibilities, one will be so far off the mark as to not even be considerable, one will be too much of a give-me to be true, and you are left with two possibilities that you must choose between. For example:

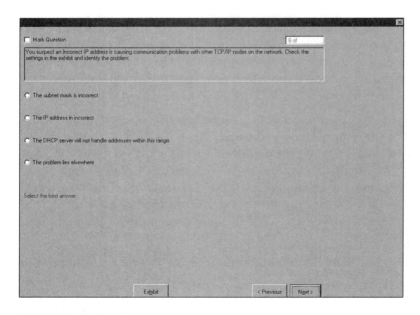

FIGURE 9.1
A sample test question.

1. In NT Server 4.0, to view the Application log, what tool must you use:

A. Application Viewer

B. Event Viewer

C. Event Observer

D. Performance Monitor

In this case, choice A is the give-me of a non-existent tool that fits the question too perfectly. Choice D is the blow-off answer so far away from what's possible as to not be considered. That leaves choices B and C to choose from.

Even if you knew nothing about NT Server at all, a clue that B and C are legitimate possibilities is the closeness in wording of each. Anytime you see two possibilities worded so closely, assume them to be the ones to focus on.

The buttons at the bottom of the screen allow you to move to the next question, or to a previous question. The latter is important because if you ever come across a question where the wording provides the answer to a question you were asked before, *always* use the previous button to go back and change or check your first answer. Never walk away from a sure thing.

If there is an exhibit associated with the question, the command button for it will be displayed as well. The problem with exhibits is that they layer on top of the question, or can be tiled in such a way that you can't see either. Whenever you have an exhibit, read the question carefully, open the exhibit, memorize what is there (or scribble information about it on your two sheets of paper), close the exhibit, and answer the question.

Figure 9.2 shows an example of a question with more than one correct answer—a fact obvious by check boxes appearing to the left of the choices instead of radio buttons.

There are two types of these questions—one where you are told how many answers are correct (choose 2, choose 3, and so on) and the other where you are not. In the example shown, you are told to choose all correct answers, and do not know if that is 2, 3, or 4. The only thing you do know is that it is not 1 and not 5—Microsoft will not use check boxes if radio boxes will work, and will never have an all of the above question.

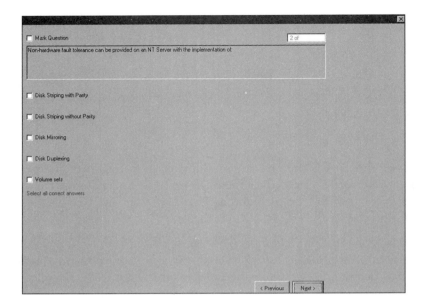

FIGURE 9.2
Another sample test question.

The vast majority of multiple answer questions offer four possibilities, meaning you must choose 2 or 3, but five possibilities (as in the figure) are not uncommon. With these questions, read the question as carefully as possible, and begin eliminating choices. For example, the question in Figure 9.2 specifically says non-hardware and one of the choices is duplexing. Duplexing requires a hardware enhancement over mirroring, so choice D is not correct. You are now left with four possibilities, and must rely upon your knowledge to choose the right ones.

The biggest problem with multiple answers is that there is no such thing as partial credit. If you are supposed to choose 4 items, and choose only 3, the question still counts as being wrong. If you should choose 2, pick one right answer, and one wrong answer, you missed the whole question. Spend much more time with multiple answer questions than single answer questions, and always come back, if time allows, after the exam and reread them carefully.

After you complete the exam, if there is time remaining, you come to an item review section, similar to that shown in Figure 9.3.

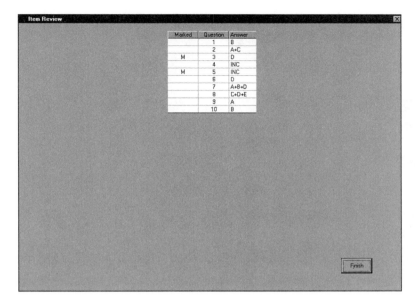

FIGURE 9.3
The Item Review at the completion of the exam.

From here you can see the questions that you marked and jump back to them. If you've already chosen an answer on that screen, it remains chosen until you choose something else (the question also remains marked until you unmark it). The command buttons at the bottom of the question will now include an Item Review choice to let you jump back to the item review screen without going through additional questions.

Use the ability to mark and jump as much as you possibly can. All lengthy questions should be marked and returned to in this manner. Also note all answers that are incomplete. You can't afford to leave any questions unanswered, so be certain to go back and fill them in before choosing to finish the exam (or running out of time).

After you click Finish, the exam is graded and the Examination Score Report appears. The one shown in Figure 9.4 is a bit misleading. Typically, only the bar graphs and a message about whether you passed or failed appear. The Section Analysis does not appear on the screen, but only on the printed documentation you walk out of the testing center with. The pass/fail score is passed on the beta of the exam, and statistics gathered from the performance of those who partook in it.

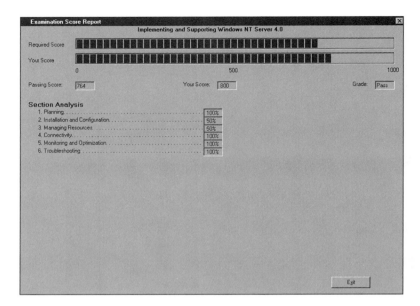

FIGURE 9.4
The Examination Score Report.

If you fail an exam, and everyone will occasionally, *never* be lulled into a false sense of confidence by the Section Analysis. If it says you scored 100% in a particular section, you should still study that section before retaking the exam. Too many test-takers study only the sections they did poorly on. That 100% in Monitoring and Optimization could be the result of the first question pool containing only one question and you had a 25% chance of guessing it correctly. What happens next time when there are three questions in the random pool from that objective category, and you don't know the answers? You're handicapping yourself right off the bat.

A good rule of thumb if you do fail an exam is to rush back to your car as quickly as you can and write down all of the questions that you can remember. Have your study materials in the vehicle with you and look up the answers then and there. If you wait until later, you'll forget many of them.

The new policy from Microsoft allows you to retake an exam you fail once without any waiting period (other than registering for it, and so on). If you fail it again, however, you must wait 14 days before you can retake it a third time (and 14 days from that point for the fourth try, and so on). This is to prevent people from actually memorizing the exam. Do your best never to fall into this category. If you fail an exam once, start all over again and study anew before trying it the second time. Make the second attempt within a week of the first, however, so that topics are fresh in your mind.

WHERE THE QUESTIONS COME FROM

Knowing where the questions come from can be as instrumental as anything in knowing how to prepare for the exam—the more you know about it, the better your odds of passing. Earlier, we discussed the time frame used to create the exam, and that contract writers are hired for the exam. The contract writers are given a sizable document detailing how questions must be written. If you really want to pursue the topic with more fervor, contact Microsoft and inquire about a contract writing position. A few tidbits that can be gleaned from multiple choice authoring, however, include the following:

1. No question should have an *All of the Above* answer. When available, this is almost always the case, and thus not a fair representation of a valid multiple choice question.

2. For the same reason, there should never be a *None of the Above* answer.

3. Scenarios should be used when they will increase the value of the question.

4. All subjective words (best, most, and so on) should be left from questions.

5. Although there can be only one correct answer for the question, all other possibilities should appear plausible, and avoid all rationale or explanations.

6. Single answers must be mutually exclusive (no A+C, B+C, and so on).

7. Negative words should be avoided (not, cannot, and so on).

DIFFERENT FLAVORS OF QUESTIONS

At one time, all questions were either single answer or multiple answer. There is a push today to go more toward *ranking* questions, and performance-based questions. Older exams still have only the first two question types, while newer ones offer the latter.

Ranking questions provide you with a scenario, a list of required objectives, a list of optional objectives, a proposed solution, and then asks you to rank how well the solution meets the objectives. A rudimentary example would be:

1. Evan is a teenager who just got his driver's license. He wants to buy a fast car and ask Betty Lou to the movies on Friday.

Required objectives:	Buy a fast car Ask Betty Lou to movies
Optional objectives:	Earn money for movies Earn money for car
Solution:	Take part-time job at the Qwik-E-Mart and buy classic '67 Cougar

Rank the solution in terms of the objectives:

A. The solution meets both required and optional objectives

B. The solution meets both required objectives and only the first optional objective

C. The solution meets both required objectives and only the second optional objective

D. The solution does not meet the required objectives

In this over-simplified example, the answer is D—the solution does not include asking Betty Lou to the movies so it does not meet the required objectives. With Ranking questions, it is often the case that the required objectives are needed in all but the last answer, so read the question backward, if you will, and see if the required objectives are being met. If they are not, you can answer the question quickly without reading any further and go on to the next question.

Performance-based questions have been incorporated in electronic testing for a long time; just not with Microsoft testing. If I really wanted to test and see how well you knew a product before hiring you, the best way to do so is to turn you loose with the product and tell you to do something. If you can, I'll hire you, and if you can't, I won't.

Taking that scenario into the testing center becomes difficult, first and foremost because you can't be allowed unrestricted access to the product within the confines of something (a shell) grading your actions. Secondly, the stability of the operations on most testing centers' antiquated machines is questionable at best. Finally, the amount of time allotted cannot exceed a reasonable amount or you will become exhausted, and the testing center will not be able to move as many people through each day.

The solution to many of these problems is to keep the number of performance-based questions to a minimum, and have you work with an emulator of some type. The emulator can come on the screen when you click the button and bring up something that looks like what the configuration information in the real product would be, without the time and overhead involved of bringing up the real product.

How do you prepare for performance-based questions? Know your product—plain and simple. Focus on the administrative side of it—how to add new users, sites, servers, directories, and so on, and you will have no difficulties. If you are very good at guessing multiple-choice answers, and really don't know the product at all, these questions will ferret that out. On the other hand, if you know your product extremely well, and just aren't good at multiple-choice guessing, you'll find these questions a godsend.

Regardless of your familiarity, or lack thereof, with the product, be very careful with all the performance-based questions. While the emulator can load much quicker than the actual product in question, it is still very time-consuming, and the amount of time required to answer each question is far from minute. These questions take a lot of time, and you need to budget for them accordingly.

IN THE FUTURE

The study of test delivery and grading is known as psychometrics, and a good many people are employed in this profession. Microsoft uses many of them to help with the design and implementation of its exams. It should come as no surprise (if you've any experience with other certifications, such as Novell's) that the next big push will be to adaptive testing.

Under adaptive testing, the amount of time for each exam can be reduced from 90 minutes to somewhere near 30, and the number of questions can drop from 50–70 down to 15 or so. This benefits you greatly, and allows more students to be tested each day at training centers, as well.

The premise behind adaptive testing is fairly simple: The first question you get is totally at random and pulled from a pool. Beyond that first question, every other question presented to you is somehow related to how well you answered the preceding question.

For example, suppose I want to give you a general exam on astronomy. The first question that comes up asks you how many planets there are in our solar system. You answer correctly (nine). I now ask you to name the third planet from the sun, and you also answer it correctly (Earth). I can now assume that you know your planets very well, and the next question will be about quasars. We'll do this for 15 questions, and if you answer them all correctly, I'll assume that you really know astronomy and pass you.

If, on the other hand, you answered Mars to the second question above, the next question will be about planets again—giving you a chance to redeem yourself. If you miss that one, I'll probably ask the most difficult question known to mankind about planets to see if you can get it right— if you can't, you don't know planets, thus you don't know astronomy, and you'll fail. In some versions of adaptive testing, you bomb out right then because there is no chance of redemption; on others, you are just given bogus questions for the remainder of the exam to make you feel like you're getting your money's worth, even though you are going to fail anyway.

Again, it differs per style/vendor but with most adaptive tests, if you answer the 15 questions and have not passed, but yet are very close to doing so, you can be asked additional questions. The additional questions give you the opportunity to redeem yourself and achieve a passing score.

The key to adaptive testing, besides each question's relationship to the one preceding it, is that every question has a point value associated with it. The first question presented is assumed to be of medium value. If you miss a question on a topic, the next one asked will be more difficult, and of higher point value, to allow the chance for redemption. If you answer the first correctly, the next question will be of lesser value, and lesser difficulty.

There is no item review in adaptive testing, and there is no going back to the preceding question(s). Once you answer a question, you are done with it, and you can draw a fair conclusion of how you did by whether or not the next question is on a similar topic.

Performance-based testing is in its infancy stages now at Microsoft, and should be rolled out within the year. Again, the best preparation here is to know your topic, and spend time with each question, making certain you fully understand what is being asked before answering. With performance-based testing, you are given a task to do in an emulator of the product you are testing on. You must perform the action and your performance is graded to see if you did it in the time and manner in which an administrator should.

This is an exam preparation book. It's the belief of the author and publisher that it's difficult to get too much practice with sample exam questions. There are other study materials available—books and software—that enable you to practice extensively, and we recommend that you give strong consideration to using these in some form.*

What follows in this chapter is a practice test designed to reflect the questions you'd likely be challenged with on an actual Microsoft exam. These questions tie in directly to the material covered in this book. Take note that when this exam goes to an adaptive format, the number of questions, passing score, and minutes necessary to take this exam will vary.

Please see the end matter of this book for more information on New Riders' TestPrep books and New Riders' Top Score exam preparation software, among other New Riders' certification study resources.

CHAPTER 10

Sample Test Questions

QUESTIONS

Please note: When this exam goes to an adaptive format, the number of questions, passing score, and minutes given to take the exam will vary.

This sample test has 60 questions, just like the actual exam, and covers each of the seven objective categories.

1. *Kristin is the NT administrator for D S Consulting—a small company with only one server, ALIEN. She has been told to implement an IIS 4 intranet, and enable anonymous access. What is the name of the WWW anonymous account, assuming defaults are used?*

   A. Administrator
   B. Anonymous
   C. IUSR_ALIEN
   D. IUSR_D
   E. IUSR_D_S_CONSULTING

2. *Evan has become very concerned about security at his site since several newspapers have been running reports about WWW break-ins. His boss is even more worried and tells him to implement the use of certificates NOW if not sooner. Which utility in Internet Service Manager is used for the requesting of certificates?*

   A. Certificate Manager
   B. Site Manager
   C. Key Manager
   D. Certificate Lord

3. *The scoundrels in Tech Support have been accessing machines they should not at other sites within Synergy Corporation and wreaking havoc. It is decided that no one coming from the Tech Support server should be allowed access to the Web server. How should access to that server be denied, assuming a single domain (select the best answer)?*

   A. by IP address
   B. by domain name
   C. by user
   D. by certificate

4. *To alleviate security concerns, you decide to use Windows NT Challenge/Response as your method of authentication. Which browsers can now access your site?*
   A. Explorer 2.0
   B. Netscape 2.0
   C. Explorer 3.0
   D. Netscape 3.0

5. *Which NTFS permission assigns the ability to read and execute only?*
   A. Full Control
   B. Read
   C. Change
   D. No Access
   E. Special

6. *Secure Sockets Layer (SSL) can be used with which types of users?*
   A. specific users only
   B. anonymous users only
   C. specific or anonymous users
   D. SSL is not used with users at all

7. *On an NT server, which file can be used on a small network for the static resolution of host names to IP addresses?*
   A. HOSTS
   B. LMHOSTS
   C. DNS
   D. WINS

8. *On an NT server, which file can be used on a small network for the static resolution of NetBIOS names to IP addresses?*
   A. HOSTS
   B. LMHOSTS
   C. DNS
   D. WINS

9. *On an NT server, which service can be used on a large network for the resolution of host names to IP addresses?*
   A. HOSTS
   B. LMHOSTS
   C. DNS
   D. WINS

10. *On an NT server, which service can be used on a large network for the dynamic resolution of NetBIOS names to IP addresses?*
    A. HOSTS
    B. LMHOSTS
    C. DNS
    D. WINS

11. *Leopold is attempting to evaluate his current equipment for suitability to hosting a Web site. What is the minimum monitor requirement of IIS 4?*
    A. CGA
    B. VGA
    C. SVGA
    D. XGA

12. *If the WWW home directory is a redirection to a share on another computer, you must give the UNC to that share. UNC is an acronym for:*
    A. Universal Naming Convention
    B. Universally Named Computer
    C. Unilateral Naming Convention
    D. Unilaterally Named Computer

13. *Which of the following is an example of a UNC?*
    A. \\server\share
    B. //server/share
    C. \\share\server
    D. //share/server

14. *Tony is setting up an IIS server (and NT) completely from scratch, and has no experience with this at all. In so doing, he has run across a number of different ways of referencing his computer. One of these is as 192.2.2.5. This is an example of:*

    A. FQDN
    B. MAC address
    C. IP address
    D. NetBIOS name

15. *Another way Tony has found to reference his computer is FF-FF-FF-FF. This is an example of:*

    A. FQDN
    B. MAC address
    C. IP address
    D. NetBIOS name

16. *In a much simpler fashion, Tony can reference his computer as D_S_Server. This is best an example of:*

    A. FQDN
    B. MAC address
    C. IP address
    D. NetBIOS name

17. *Finally, Tony can also reference his computer as www.roguemdc.com. This is his:*

    A. FQDN
    B. MAC address
    C. IP address
    D. NetBIOS name

18. *Landon James has just finished adding the FTP service to his IIS 4.0 server. What directory was created during the installation of this service?*

    A. \ftp
    B. \ftproot
    C. \rootftp
    D. No additional directory was created.

19. *What directory access control must Landon James add to a directory for an FTP user to be able to download files from that directory?*

    A. Execute
    B. Read
    C. Create
    D. Modify
    E. Change

20. *Bandwidth is a major issue for Mckenzie. Her LAN users are complaining that they are being denied access to server files since the server became the WWW host. To better serve her LAN users, Mckenzie should implement:*

    A. HTTP Keep-Alives
    B. Bandwidth choking
    C. Limited connections
    D. Bandwidth throttling
    E. User logon requirements

21. *IIS 4.0 configuration values, for the most part, are stored in memory where?*

    A. text files
    B. Access databases
    C. The Registry
    D. IIS Metabase
    E. Information Store

22. *The tool used to remotely manage your Web site using a standard Internet browser is:*

    A. Internet Service Manager (HTML)
    B. MMC
    C. Content Analyzer
    D. Server Manager

23. *Rob fears that his NT server that is hosting his IIS site is acting up. He needs to check the system log to verify his hunches. What tool can he use to check the system log?*

    A. Any text editor
    B. Internet Service Manager
    C. MMC
    D. Event Viewer

24. The default subnet mask assigned to an IP address of 100.100.100.200 is:

    A. 0.0.0.0

    B. 255.0.0.0

    C. 255.255.0.0

    D. 255.255.255.0

25. How can you test the installation of an FTP server?

    A. Ping the FTP loopback address.

    B. Ping another FTP server.

    C. FTP another server.

    D. FTP the loopback address.

26. In the DNS name www.amazon.com, *what does* amazon *represent?*

    A. The last name of the host

    B. The domain in which the host is located

    C. The IP address of the building in which the host is located

    D. The directory in which the host name file is located

27. Jack is a consultant called in to advise McBride, Inc. on how to set up its Web site. It wants to use IIS in a way that users must give a valid username and password to gain access. All the users are using the latest version of Explorer as their browser. Which authentication method should Jack recommend?

    A. Basic Text

    B. Any authentication method

    C. NT Challenge/Response

    D. SSL

28. What FTP permission is needed for users to be able to upload files to a directory?

    A. Write

    B. Execute

    C. Read

    D. Change

    E. Modify

29. *Jane is attempting to alter the TCP port assignments on her server to hide several services. The default port for SSL is:*

    A. 21

    B. 25

    C. 80

    D. 110

    E. 443

30. *Jane knows that she definitely wants to hide the WWW service. The default port for it is:*

    A. 21

    B. 25

    C. 80

    D. 110

    E. 443

31. *What is the maximum number of SMTP simultaneous connections allowed by default?*

    A. 10

    B. 500

    C. 1000

    D. 5000

32. *Jenna needs to get to the SMTP property sheets to make modifications. These are accessed via:*

    A. SMTP Manager

    B. Internet Service Manager

    C. The Control Panel—SMTP icon

    D. The Setup utility for IIS

33. *The default number of inactive seconds before an SMTP disconnect is:*

    A. 30

    B. 60

    C. 600

    D. 900

    E. 999

34. *Mary Kay is using SSL and NNTP. Assuming no changes have been made manually, what is the default TCP port that NNTP is using?*

    A. 25

    B. 80

    C. 119

    D. 563

35. *Mary Kay has stopped using SSL because there is not a need at her small site (which does not offer outside access). Assuming no changes have been manually made, what is the TCP port assignment NNTP is using?*

    A. 25

    B. 80

    C. 119

    D. 563

36. *When Daisha creates a new newsgroup by the name Friday, NNTP will automatically create a new directory to hold the articles. The name of the directory will be:*

    A. Friday.nntp

    B. Friday.xix

    C. Friday.nws

    D. Friday

    E. Daisha

37. *How many articles can a single NNTP index hold?*

    A. unlimited

    B. 256

    C. 128

    D. NNTP articles are not indexed

38. *Alana has just installed the NNTP service on her server, and used the default settings to do so. What directory was created during the installation?*

    A. %SystemRoot%\System32\NNTP

    B. %SystemRoot%\Innetpub\NNTP

    C. %SystemRoot%\Innetpub\NNTPROOT

    D. %SystemRoot%\System32\NNTPROOT

    E. No additional directories are created.

39. *Michael is trying to find the MIME mappings for his site. Where are they stored?*

    A. in text files
    B. in .XIX files
    C. in the Registry
    D. in the metabase
    E. in the MIME Manager

40. *Hannah has elected to create FTP log files to keep track of the traffic she is getting. Where can she find these files as they are created?*

    A. %SystemRoot%\Innetpub\Logfiles
    B. \Logfiles
    C. %SystemRoot%\System32\Logfiles
    D. \etc

41. *Which of the following operators can be used in .HTX files?*

    A. CONTAINS
    B. INCLUDES
    C. EQ
    D. MT

42. *Which of the following files is responsible for providing ODBC functionality in IIS?*

    A. HTTP.API
    B. HTTP.DLL
    C. HTTPODBC.API
    D. HTTPODBC.DLL

43. *Which parameter should Evan use in his .IDC file to truncate entries that exceed a certain size?*

    A. MaxRecords
    B. MaxFieldSize
    C. TruncateSize
    D. MaxTruncateSize
    E. MaxRecordSize

44. *After a query has been processed by Index Server, the results are sent to what type of file to use as a template for formatting the result?*

    A. TMX
    B. IDQ
    C. TEM
    D. HTM
    E. HTX

45. *As input, Index Server uses files with what extension?*

    A. TMX
    B. IDQ
    C. TEM
    D. HTM
    E. HTX

46. *Arthur is trying to determine what permissions are needed on IDQ files for them to function properly. Which two of the following are correct?*

    A. Script
    B. Execute
    C. Read
    D. Write
    E. Change

47. *Which of the following tags are optional in an IDQ file?*

    A. [Query]
    B. [Query Detail]
    C. [BeginDetail]
    D. [Names]

48. *How many characters can be used in the path specification for a template?*

    A. unlimited
    B. 260
    C. 256
    D. 255
    E. 8

49. *Which of the following files can contain queries?*

A. HTX

B. HTM

C. IDC

D. IDQ

50. *Which character would be used in a script file to prevent that line from being processed?*

A. +

B. %

C. @

D. #

51. *Tracy is trying to find the* Cscript *parameter used to save the current command line for the user. It is:*

A. //C

B. //I

C. //B

D. //S

E. //R

52. *Tracy is now trying to find the* Cscript *parameter used to register script extensions. It is:*

A. //C

B. //I

C. //B

D. //S

E. //R

53. *Jeff is debating whether to use CGI or ISAPI to write the scripts he needs. What are the advantages of ISAPI over CGI?*

A. It is loaded into memory at startup.

B. It runs as a TSR.

C. It is reusable.

D. It runs as a DLL.

54. *Which of the following is true of Active Server Pages?*

A. They must have .ASP extensions.

B. They can have any extension.

C. They can contain standard HTML tags.

D. They cannot contain standard HTML tags.

55. *Ardith is selecting WWW log files to be created based upon size, rather than date, month, and so on. What is the default file size used?*

   A. 1MB
   B. 9MB
   C. 19MB
   D. 91MB

56. *In which file would an administrator be most likely to find the* MaxRecords *parameter?*

   A. System.idc
   B. System.idq
   C. System.htx
   D. System.htm

57. *In which file would an administrator be most likely to find the* CiCodePage *parameter?*

   A. System.idc
   B. System.idq
   C. System.htx
   D. System.htm

58. *Active Server tags begin with what character(s)?*

   A. [
   B. <
   C. %
   D. <%
   E. [%

59. *Active Server tags are also known as?*

   A. Primary script commands
   B. Loops
   C. DLLs
   D. Conditional Executives

60. *Linda is trying to find a command-line scripting host, and James insists that one came with IIS. What is the name of the command-line scripting host?*

   A. Wscript
   B. Sscript
   C. Cscript
   D. Cnscript

ANSWERS AND EXPLANATIONS

1. **C** IUSR_ALIEN would be the default anonymous account user name, by default, on the ALIEN server.

2. **C** Key Manager is used to request certificates.

3. **A** The best solution would be to disallow access to the server by IP address.

4. **A - C** Explorer 2.0 or later is required for Windows NT Challenge/Response authentication.

5. **B** The Read permission would allow for read and execute.

6. **C** SSL works with specific or anonymous users.

7. **A** The HOSTS file is used for static host name to IP address resolution.

8. **B** The LMHOSTS file is used for static NetBIOS name to IP address resolution.

9. **C** DNS is used for host name to IP address resolution on large networks.

10. **D** WINS is used for dynamic NetBIOS name to IP address resolution.

11. **C** An SVGA monitor is required for IIS 4.

12. **A** UNC is an acronym for Universal Naming Convention.

13. **A** \\server\share is an example of a UNC.

14. **C** 192.2.2.5 is an example of an IP address.

15. **B** FF-FF-FF-FF is an example of a MAC address.

16. **D** D_S_Server is an example of a NetBIOS name.

17. **A** www.roguemdc.com is an example of a Fully Qualified Domain Name (FQDN).

18. **B** The \ftproot directory is created during the installation of the FTP service.

19. **B** The user must have Read access to be able to download files in FTP.

20. **D** Bandwidth throttling will reduce the amount of bandwidth available to the WWW service.

21. **D** The metabase stores memory-resident values about IIS.

22. **A** The tool used to remotely manage your Web site using a standard Internet browser is Internet Service Manger (HTML).

23. **D** Event Viewer is used to check the system log.

24. **B** The default subnet mask assigned to an IP address of 100.100.100.200 is 255.0.0.0.

25. **D** You can test the installation of an FTP server by FTP'ing the loopback address.

26. **B** The path specifies a host named www in a domain amazon. The domain amazon is located in the top-level domain com.

27. **C** Jack should recommend NT Challenge/Response.

28. **A** The FTP Write permission is needed for users to be able to upload files to a directory.

29. **E** The default port for SSL is 443.

30. **C** The default port for WWW is 80.

31. **C** The maximum number of SMTP simultaneous connections allowed by default is 1000.

32. **B** SMTP property sheets are accessed via Internet Service Manager.

33. **C** The default number of inactive seconds before an SMTP disconnect is 600.

34. **D** NNTP with SSL uses TCP port 563.

35. **C**   NNTP without SSL uses port 119.

36. **D**   A new newsgroup by the name Friday will automatically create a new directory named Friday.

37. **C**   A single NNTP index can hold 128 article entries.

38. **C**   Installing NNTP creates the %SystemRoot%\Innetpub\ NNTPROOT directory.

39. **C**   MIME mappings are stored in the Registry.

40. **C**   FTP log files are in %SystemRoot%\System32\Logfiles.

41. **A - C**   .HTX files operators include EQ and CONTAINS.

42. **D**   ODBC functionality in IIS is provided by HTTPODBC.DLL.

43. **B**   The MaxFieldSize parameter determines when to truncate entries that exceed a certain size.

44. **E**   After a query has been processed by Index Server, the results are sent to an .HTX file to use as a template for formatting the result.

45. **B**   As input, Index Server uses files with an IDQ extension.

46. **A - B**   Execute and Script permissions are required on IDQ files for proper usage.

47. **D**   The [Names] tag is optional in an IDQ file.

48. **B**   260 characters can be used in the path specification for a template.

49. **C - D**   IDC and IDQ files can contain queries.

50. **D**   The # character should be used in a script file to prevent that line from being processed.

51. **D**   /SS is the Cscript parameter used to save the current command line for the user.

52. **E** //R is the Cscript parameter used to register script extensions.

53. **A - C - D** ISAPI is loaded into memory at startup, is reusable, and runs as a DLL.

54. **A - C** Active Server Pages have .ASP extensions, and can contain standard HTML tags.

55. **C** The default file size for log files is 19MB.

56. **C** MaxRecords is a parameter used in .HTX files.

57. **B** CiCodePage is a variable used in .IDQ files.

58. **D** Active Server tags begin with <%.

59. **A** Active Server tags are also known as Primary script commands.

60. **C** The command-line scripting host is Cscript.

If you feel you need to practice more exam-like questions, take a look at New Riders' MCSE Test Prep *series of certification preparation books, featuring hundreds of review questions and concise explanations of why answer choices are correct or incorrect. These books are specifically designed for exam candidates who want to drill themselves extensively on exam questions.*

The breadth and depth of your technical vocabulary is a significant measure of your knowledge as applied to the exam you're about to be tested on. The hotlist of exam-critical concepts is something you should access every time you run across a term or a word you're not sure about. Double-check your knowledge by reviewing this section from time to time; do you have a slightly different definition for a term? Why? The answer can deepen your understanding of the technology.

Do you need to add your own definitions or new terms? It's more than likely, since no two exam candidates will find the same list of terms equally useful. That's why there's room to add your own terms and concepts at the end of this section.

CHAPTER 11

Hotlist of Exam-Critical Concepts

Term	*Definition*
ACK	Acknowledgment—A response from a receiving computer to a sending computer to indicate successful reception of information. TCP requires that packets are acknowledged before it considers the transmission safe.
Active open	An action taken by a client to initiate a TCP connection with a server.
address classes	Grouping of IP addresses with each class, defining the maximum number of networks and hosts available. The first octet of the address determines the class.
address mask	A 32-bit binary number used to select bits from an IP address for subnet masking.
analog	A form of electronic communication using a continuous electromagnetic wave, such as television or radio. Any continuous wave form as opposed to digital on/off transmissions.
ANSI	American National Standards Institute— The membership organization responsible for defining U.S. standards in the information technology industry.
API	Application Programming Interface—A language and message format that enables a programmer to use functions in another program or in the hardware.
ARP	Address Resolution Protocol—A protocol in the TCP/IP suite used to bind an IP address to a physical hardware address.
ARPA	Advanced Research Projects Agency—a government agency that originally funded the research on the ARPANET (became DARPA in the mid-1970s).

Term	*Definition*
ARPANET	The first network of computers funded by the U.S. Department of Defense Advanced Projects Agency. An experimental communications network funded by the government that eventually developed into the Internet.
ASCII	Data that is limited to letters, numbers, and punctuation.
ATM	Asynchronous Transfer Mode—A broadband networking technology.
backbone	Generally very high-speed, T3 telephone lines that connect remote ends of networks and networks to one another; only service providers are connected to the Internet in this way.
baseband	A network technology that requires all nodes attached to the network to participate in every transmission. Ethernet, for example, is a baseband technology.
BOOTP	Bootstrap Protocol—A protocol used to configure systems across internetworks with an IP address, subnet mask and a default gateway.
bps	bits per second—A measurement that expresses the speed at which data is transferred between computers.
bridge	A device that connects one physical section of a network to another, often providing isolation.
broadband	A network technology that multiplexes multiple network carriers into a single cable.

Term	*Definition*
broadcast	A packet destined for all hosts on the network.
brouter	A computer device that works as both a bridge and a router. Some network traffic may be bridged while some is routed.
buffer	A storage area used to hold input or output data.
checksumming	A service performed by UDP that checks to see if packets were changed during transmission.
connectionless service	A delivery service that treats each packet as a separate entity. Often results in lost packets or packets delivered out of sequence.
CRC	Cyclic Redundancy Check—A computation about a frame of which the result is a small integer. The value is appended to the end of the frame and recalculated when the frame is received. If the results differ from the appended value, the frame has presumably been corrupted and is therefore discarded. It is used to detect errors in transmission.
CSMA	Carrier Sense Multiple Access—A simple media access control protocol that enables multiple stations to contend for access to the medium. If no traffic is detected on the medium, the station may send a transmission.
CSMA/CD	Carrier Sense Multiple Access with Collision Detection—A characteristic of network hardware that uses CSMA in conjunction with a process that detects when two stations transmit simultaneously. If that happens, both back off and retry the transmission after a random time period has elapsed.

Term	*Definition*
DARPA	Defense Advanced Research Projects Agency, originally ARPA—The government agency that funded the research that developed the ARPANET.
datagram	A packet of data and delivery information.
DHCP	Dynamic Host Configuration Protocol—A protocol that provides dynamic address allocation and automatic TCP/IP configuration.
digital	Type of communications used by computers, consisting of individual on and off pulses. Compare to analog.
directed broadcast address	An IP address that specifies all hosts on the network.
domain	Highest subdivision of the Internet, for the most part by country (except in the U.S., where it's by type of organization, such as educational, commercial, and government). Usually the last part of a host name; for example, the domain part of ibm.com is .com, which represents the domain of commercial sites in the U.S.
Domain Name System (DNS)	The system that translates between Internet IP address and Internet host names.
Ethernet	A type of local area network hardware. Many TCP/IP networks are Ethernet based.
FDDI	Fiber Distributed Data Interface
FDM	Frequency Division Multiplexing—A technique of passing signals across a single medium by assigning each signal a unique carrier frequency.

Term	*Definition*
firewall	A device placed on a network to prevent unauthorized traffic from entering the network.
FQDN	Fully Qualified Domain Name—A combination of the host name and the domain name.
frame	Packets as transmitted across a medium. Differing frame types have unique characteristics.
frame relay	A type of digital data communications protocol.
FTP	File Transfer Protocol—A popular Internet communications protocol that allows you to transfer files between hosts on the Internet.
gateway	A device that interfaces two networks using different protocols.
hardware address	The physical address of a host used by networks.
host	A server using TCP/IP, and/or connected to the Internet.
host address	A unique number assigned to identify a host on the Internet (also called IP address or dot address). This address is usually represented as four numbers between 1 and 255 and separated by periods, for example, 192.58.107.230.
host ID	The portion of an IP address that identifies the host in a particular network. It is used in conjunction with network IDs to form a complete IP address.

Term	*Definition*
host name	A unique name for a host that corresponds to the host address.
HTML	Hypertext Markup Language—The formatting language/protocol used to define various text styles in a hypertext document, including emphasis and bulleted lists.
HTTP	Hypertext Transfer Protocol—The communications protocol used by WWW services to retrieve documents quickly.
ICMP	Internet Control Message Protocol—A maintenance protocol that handles error messages to be sent when datagrams are discarded or when systems experience congestion.
IGMP	Internet Group Management Protocol—A protocol used to carry group membership information in a multicast system.
ISDN	Integrated Services Digital Network—A dedicated telephone line connection that transmits digital data at the rate of 64 to 128Kbps.
LAN	Local Area Network—A network of computers that is usually limited to a small physical area, like a building.
LLC	Logical Link Control—A protocol that provides a common interface point to the MAC layers.
MAC	Media Access Control—A protocol that governs the access method a station has to the network.
MAN	Metropolitan Area Network—A physical communications network that operates across a metropolitan area.

Term	*Definition*
MIME	A protocol that describes the format of Internet messages (Multipurpose Internet Mail Extension)
name resolution	The process of mapping a computer name to an IP address. DNS and DHCP are two ways of resolving names.
NFS	Network File System—A file system developed by Sun Microsystems that is now widely used on many different networks.
NIC	Network Interface Card—An add-on card to allow a machine to access a LAN (most commonly an Ethernet card).
nodes	Individual computers connected to a network.
OSI	Open Systems Interconnection—A set of ISO standards that define the framework for implementing protocols in seven layers.
packet	The unit of data transmission on the Internet. A packet consists of the data being transferred with additional overhead information, such as transmitting and receiving addresses.
packet switching	The communications technology that the Internet is based on, where data being sent between computers is transmitted in packets.
Ping	A utility that sends out a packet to an Internet host and waits for a response (used to check whether a host is up).
POP	Point of Presence—Indicates availability of a local access number to a public data network.

Term	*Definition*
PPP	Point-to-Point Protocol—A driver that enables you to use a network communications protocol over a phone line, used with TCP/IP to allow you to have a dial-in Internet host.
PPTP	Point-to-Point-Tunneling Protocol—A newer version of PPP used to create Virtual Private Networks.
protocol	The standard that defines how computers on a network communicate with one another.
RARP	Reverse Address Resolution Protocol—A protocol that enables a computer to find its IP address by broadcasting a request. It is usually used by diskless workstations at startup to find their logical IP address.
repeater	Device that enables you to extend the length of your network by amplifying and repeating the information it receives.
RIP	Routing Information Protocol—A router-to-router protocol used to exchange information between routers. RIP supports dynamic routing.
router	Equipment that receives an Internet packet and sends it to the next machine in the destination path.
segment	Protocol data unit consisting of part of a stream of bytes being sent between two machines. It also includes information about the current position in the stream and a checksum value.
server	Provider of a service—A computer that runs services. It also often refers to a piece of hardware or software that provides access to information requested from it.

Term	*Definition*
service	Application that processes requests by client applications; for example, storing data or executing an algorithm.
SLIP	Serial Line Internet Protocol—A way of running TCP/IP via the phone lines to allow you to have a dialup Internet host.
SMTP	Simple Mail Transport Protocol—The accepted communications protocol standard for exchange of email between Internet hosts.
SNA	System Network Architecture—A protocol suite developed and used by IBM.
SNMP	Simple Network Management Protocol—A communications protocol used to control and monitor devices on a network.
socket	A means of network communications via special entities.
subnet	Any lower network that is part of the logical network—identified by the network ID.
subnet mask	A 32-bit value that distinguishes the network ID from the host ID in an IP address.
TCP/IP	Transmission Control Protocol/Internet Protocol—A communications protocol suite that allows computers of any make to communicate when running TCP/IP software.
TFTP	Trivial File Transfer Protocol—A basic, standard protocol used to upload or download files with minimal overhead. TFTP depends on UDP and is often used to initialize diskless workstations, as it has no directory and password capabilities.

Term	*Definition*
transceiver	A device that connects a host interface to a network. It is used to apply signals to the cable and sense collisions.
UDP	User Datagram Protocol—A simple protocol that enables an application program on one machine to send a datagram to an application program on another machine. Delivery is not guaranteed, nor is it guaranteed the datagrams will be delivered in proper order.
URL	Universal Resource Locator—A means of specifying the location of information on the Internet for WWW clients.
WAN	Wide area network—A network of computers that are geographically dispersed.
X.25	A CCITT standard for connecting computers to a network that provides a reliable stream transmission service, which can support remote logins.
X.400	A CCITT standard for message transfer and interpersonal messaging, like electronic mail.

Additional Terms and Concepts

_____

_____

_____

_____

_____

_____

_____

_____

Not every interesting item the instructor has to share with the class is neccesarily related directly to the exam. That's the case with "Did You Know?" Think of the information in here as the intriguing sidebar, or the interesting diversion, you might wish the instructor would share with you during an aside.

CHAPTER 12

Did You Know?

The following are interesting items not relevant to the exam:

1. A number of items regarding IIS can be tweaked through the Registry. Entries for the Web service are listed in Table 12.1 Settings relevant to IIS are under the following Registry path:

   HKEY_LOCAL_MACHINE\SYSTEM\CurrentControlSet\ Services\W3SVC\Parameters

2. The Microsoft Management Console included with IIS on the NT Option Pack is scheduled to be the new administrative tool throughout the whole BackOffice suite. Each product in the suite will include its own snap-in that will work within MMC.

3. If you have users using the desktop on machines with IIS installed, you can restrict their ability to alter services by renaming .CPL files (Control Panel applets).

4. IIS 4.0 is the first version of IIS to allow synchronization of password changes between NT and IIS.

5. For special offers you have available on your Web site, configure an expiration time for headers. On each request, the date is checked to see if the header should be displayed, or if its time has expired.

TABLE 12.1

REGISTRY ENTRIES FOR THE WEB SERVICE

Property	Data Type	Default Setting	Range Value	Description
AcceptByteRanges	REG_DWORD	1 (enabled)	1, 0	When enabled, the Web server sends the Accept-Range:bytes header field to accept range requests.
AllowGuestAccess	REG_DWORD	1 (enabled)	1, 0	Enables guest services on the service. This entry is available for the FTP service (MSFTPSVC) as well. Change this entry to 0 to disable guest access on your server.
AllowSpecialChars InShell	REG_DWORD	0 (disabled)	1, 0	Enables batch files (.BAT and .CMD) to use special characters to be used, including ; ,	(% and <>. Keep this setting to 0 to reduce the threat of users using these characters to hack into your site. If you enable this setting, users can pass these characters (except | and <>) to CGI scripts. When disabled, however, users cannot send these characters to CGI scripts.
DLCCookieNameString	REG_STRING	none	string	Denotes the cookie string that is sent to down-level clients.
DLCHostNameString	REG_STRING	none	string	Specifies the Web site name where the down level host menu document is stored. You can find the downlevel host menu name by looking at the DLCCookieMenuDocumentString Registry entry.

continues

TABLE 12.1 continued

Property	Data Type	Default Setting	Range Value	Description
DLCCookieMenu-DocumentString	REG_STRING	none	string	Indicates the host menu file name for clients that do not support HOST header but that support cookies.
DLCMungeMenu-DocumentString	REG_STRING	none	string	Indicates the host menu file name for clients that do not support cookies.
DLCMenuString	REG_STRING	none	string	Specifies the special prefix of URLs requested by downlevel clients.
DLCSupport	REG_DWORD	0 (disabled)	1, 0	Enables downlevel client support.
EnableSvcLoc	REG_DWORD	1 (enabled)	1, 0	Registers IIS services so the Internet Service Manager can locate the service. This entry is supported by the FTP service as well.
* LanguageEngines	REG_STRING	none	string	Specifies a scripting language that does not support the Active Server Pages Object.Method syntax.
LogErrorRequests	REG_DWORD	1 (enabled)	1, 0	Enables or disables error logging.
LogSuccessRequests	REG_DWORD	1 (enabled)	1, 0	Enables or disables the logging of successful activities.
SSIEnableCmd-Direct	REG_DWORD	1 (enabled)	1, 0	Setting this value to 0 increases security for sites that want to disable the #exec cmd directive of server-side includes when shell commands are executed.

Property	Data Type	Default Setting	Range Value	Description
TryExceptDisable	REG_DWORD	0 (disabled)	1, 0	When ISAPI applications run, this setting enables or disables exception caching when HttpExtensionproc() is called. Set this entry to 1 when you want to perform JIT debugging. Otherwise, set to 0 so ISAPI applications do not bring the server down in the event of an error in the ISAPI application.
UploadReadAhead	REG_DWORD	48KB	0-0x80000000	Specifies the default amount of data posted by a client that the server reads before passing control to the application. Higher values require more server RAM.

*To use the LanguageEngines entry, you must create the following key under the W3SVC key: \ASP\LanguageEntries\Name_of_Language

INDEX

How to Contact Us

IF YOU NEED THE LATEST UPDATES ON A TITLE THAT YOU'VE PURCHASED:

1) Visit our Web site at www.newriders.com.

2) Click on the DOWNLOADS link, and enter your book's ISBN number, which is located on the back cover in the bottom right-hand corner.

3) In the DOWNLOADS section, you'll find available updates that are linked to the book page.

IF YOU ARE HAVING TECHNICAL PROBLEMS WITH THE BOOK OR THE CD THAT IS INCLUDED:

1) Check the book's information page on our Web site according to the instructions listed above, or

2) Email us at support@mcp.com, or

3) Fax us at (317) 817-7488 attn: Tech Support.

IF YOU HAVE COMMENTS ABOUT ANY OF OUR CERTIFICATION PRODUCTS THAT ARE NON-SUPPORT RELATED:

1) Email us at certification@mcp.com, or

2) Write to us at New Riders, 201 W. 103rd St., Indianapolis, IN 46290-1097, or

3) Fax us at (317) 581-4663.

IF YOU ARE OUTSIDE THE UNITED STATES AND NEED TO FIND A DISTRIBUTOR IN YOUR AREA:

Please contact our international department at international@mcp.com.

IF YOU WISH TO PREVIEW ANY OF OUR CERTIFICATION BOOKS FOR CLASSROOM USE:

Email us at pr@mcp.com. Your message should include your name, title, training company or school, department, address, phone number, office days/hours, text in use, and enrollment. Send these details along with your request for desk/examination copies and/or additional information.